`DETERMINED TO DISCOVER WHY?

By Marian Brown

ISBN: 978-1-7376250-0-1

Printed in the United States of America

TABLE OF CONTENTS

Acknowledgements

First, I want to give thanks to God Almighty. His Holy Spirit allowed me to see I have a story inside me that's able to mend hearts broken by unforgiveness, bitterness, and pain. A special thanks to my elder brother, Jr, who not only led me by the hand when we were little but introduced me to Jesus Christ out of genuine love and concern for my spiritual welfare. To my sons and grandchildren who have been the light on my shoulders. Thank you! Many thanks to Tanja, Alice, Joyce, Carol, Pumpkin, Michael, SDB, Pam, and Patricia. I shared my idea with them. Thirteen years later, a special thanks to Jerome Curry who connected me to Robyn Norwood, an amazing young woman of God who created a path to propel me to completion with her selfless skills and connections. I am eternally grateful for those of you that were used as instruments in my growth to make this day happen.

DEDICATION

In memory of my dad, who was my hero, and my mother, who was the epitome of a godly woman of service.

In memory of Ermenine Reynolds, Wiley Porter, Mildred Johnson, Mechile Davis, Tometha Faulk, Andre Jimmersion and Henry White. Lastly, I want to dedicate this book to every young woman who feels stuck and has been tempted to give up.

SPECIAL MESSAGE

Quitting is not an option! God made no mistakes when you were created. Everything that touches your life is by his design.

You can handle it, otherwise you wouldn't have made it this far. Block thoughts like: it's too late, I can't make it, I've gone too far and no one will forgive or trust me, I'm too old, I'll have to raise those children alone, no one will want me, I'm a failure, I was a beauty but look at me now, my days are almost over. I have good news for you dear sister. Be encouraged because God has plans for you. They're good, not evil, meant to heal and prosper, not harm you. And you, my brothers, it's your time to take your rightful place in the presence of the Lord. No, it's not too late. Make this the beginning of the rest of your lives. Say "I love you" to those you cherish. Say

"I'm sorry." It's the beginning of your healing, my friend. It doesn't matter if you're a pastor, lawyer, doctor, trucker, banker, salesman, professor, or businessman. We all must come the same way.

And to everyone reading this book, God has a plan for you, too. I've been in your shoes. I was brought up with four brothers, raised five sons, mentored many young women across the globe, and went from a Christian home to fornication, adultery, drugs, lying, stealing, self-righteousness, bitterness, anger, and unforgiveness just to name a few. If there was hope for me, there is hope for you. Your obstacle is huge because your purpose is even bigger. So, PUSH! Quitting is not an option.

CHAPTER 1

DETERMINED TO DISCOVER WHY?

My insecurities killed my self-esteem until God answered my every why. If you're a woman who has experienced physical, emotional, or spiritual abuse as a Christian and had greater expectations once becoming a believer, you're likely thinking "I hoped this would be better." Have you suppressed the pain of disappointment to protect those you love? The process is necessary, but just like a caterpillar who has morphed into a butterfly, you are about to soar.

I want to thank you for taking me up on this journey. Not only will I share with you my hardships and the emotions I've experienced, but I'll assist you in a step-by-step method guided by the Holy Spirit in discovering there are no limitations when it comes to God. He says who you are and where He is taking you. I'll assist you in discovering the root of your pain and facing it head on. If you follow the steps with a sincere and humble heart, you'll be on your way to fulling your destiny.

To move forward, you must face your past. I'll show you how to embrace it. You'll see why some people were removed from your life. You'll be able to identify the three types of people placed in your life and avoid emotional disturbances when they disappear. You'll discover how each obstacle you face is preparation for your future.

Since I was twelve, my mother encouraged me to express myself through journaling. I wrote about what I was going to be and what was happening around me. Even when I was being disobedient, I would write about it. I journaled about my favorite subjects in

school—science and theater—and my dream of
becoming wealthy as a model or entrepreneur. As I
journaled I wondered why unfortunate things would
happen to me.

My fortitude propelled me to never give up despite my
misfortunes. I searched for my worth in others, trying
to be what they wanted me to be. Today, I'm an
entrepreneur assisting families financially across the U.S.
I'm doing what I love to do: empowering others
through my work as a certified evangelism trainer, life
coach, and philanthropist. Thirteen years ago, I realized
I should tell my story to the world. Many women have
experienced the same pain of rejection and bitterness as
I have and can't break free. If you're one of those
women, my desire in sharing my story is to help you
open the prison doors of your own mind and
experience true freedom. Only FREE women can
FREE women.

WHAT THIS BOOK IS NOT

Though I'm giving you simple suggestions that will help you achieve freedom, no two people are alike. Therefore, you must carefully seek God while reading this book. It's not about religion, it's about my personal relationship with God and how He loved me even when I didn't love myself. Lastly, this book is not a substitute for counseling or therapy. Seeking help from qualified professionals may be a crucial step for many of you to overcome your hardships.

WHAT THIS BOOK IS

This book reveals my story of pain, struggle, love, betrayal, and victory. Find light and hope in these anecdotes and let them help shape you into the amazing person God created you to be.

CHAPTER 2

SALVATION

According to the scriptures, salvation is deliverance from sin and its consequences by believing Jesus died for our sins and rose from the dead on the third day.

Allow me to take you back to how I grew up and how my life was before I came to know Jesus. I have four brothers and a sister. My sister was my cousin but, through adoption, became my sister when I was about thirteen.

Mother and daddy disagreed on few things but the one thing they agreed on was a relationship with God through his Son, Jesus Christ. Mother would always say there was no better place to be found than in the house of the Lord. They never missed a beat attending church despite their differences. Staying home from church was not an option for us. We attended Sunday school, Baptist training union, bible class, and prayer meetings. Sunday was a big day for us. Whatever we had going on had to stop. It was God's Day. There was no such thing as working on Sunday, not in our house. Daddy said, "God worked six days and on the seventh he rested."

We ate breakfast every morning as a family, but Sunday morning was different. Mother would fix breakfast and we'd all gather around the table to eat after gathering in the living room as a family to pray and sing. I'd hold my brother Manny's hand who was six years younger than me, and he'd hold Pie's hand who was two years younger than him. Both of my parents' families could all sing, and if they weren't singers, they were preachers. They would still be singing, but I was ready to eat.

Good Lord! I knew they would be singing 'til Jesus came back. AMEN was my favorite word!

Off to the table we'd go. Daddy would say, "Let's bless the food."

I would be thinking, "Didn't we just bless it thirty minutes ago? Can't we just eat?" Of course, I never said it aloud.

Mother would sit in the living room after we would pray. She would drink coffee and eat an egg while we'd have grits, eggs, bacon, toast, jelly, and biscuits. I never knew why Mother only drank coffee. She never said a word until I asked her thirty years later. Her answer was, "I wanted to make sure my children and my husband were good and full." She served my dad, and she served her children.

Mother stood about 4 feet 11 inches, was mild mannered and extremely smart. Daddy was 6'2, mean as hell, and a prize fighter before he was a preacher. His motto was always "Quitting is not an option." There was never room for losing a fight.

My daddy would cuss like nobody's business when he was angry. His favorite word was "bastard." Daddy's temper was so bad we feared him almost worse than we feared the devil. When we did something wrong, he would beat us. I know the bible says "beat the child and he will not die." But dang, I don't think God meant it like that.

He would beat us so bad at times he'd draw blood. I remember once he made me find three switches. He plaited them and beat the daylights out of me. I was rebellious, but I think one switch would have been sufficient.

I felt like Cinderella most days since I was the only girl at home. Mother taught me to cook, and I'd cook for the family, scrub the house clean, and go to school and to church. I couldn't go to parties or anything like most of my friends. Today, I realize it was only for my protection. My mother knew things I didn't. She'd been places I'd never been. Once, I wanted to get out of the house so badly, I lied and said I was going to Junior Achievement (JA), a junior high school program teaching young children how to become entrepreneurs. So, mother let me go to JA on Thursdays to help cultivate the entrepreneur spirit in me.

I went to JA for only one month of the school year. The rest of those Thursday nights, my friends and I would be in the French Quarter partying. My parents weren't aware. I was exposed to so much evil at such an early age because of that. It was truly God's mercy and protection that got me through it, even though I didn't have a relationship with him back then. That's why I tell young people, "You can't slick the slicker." I've been there, done that, and have got the t-shirt.

I was always making and selling something, just like my mother and dad. I remember I use to catch all sorts of reptiles, including snakes and lizards.

Daddy saw my interest and he would bring me snakes from the country. Sounds gross, right? Yeah, but those slimy looking, smelly snakes would be for sale later. They made beautiful belts and bracelets. One time, Daddy brought a snake home for me and I skinned it, soaked the skin in formaldehyde, preserved it in salt and

laid it in the freezer on newspaper to dry out. Mother opened the freezer, saw the snake skin lying there, and screamed. She didn't usually curse, but that day she did. Guess you know I was punished, huh? Grounded was my middle name.

Mother and I were close when I was growing up. She taught me the best she knew how about sex, boys, and what to expect when that time of the month arrives. I'd ask her lots of questions and she would patiently answer them all. Mother was really good with numbers, too. I remember when she taught me how to use a checkbook at thirteen years old. None of my friends knew how. She would have me practice writing checks on paper and then enter them in her checkbook.

Mother would always tell me how much she loved me. Daddy, on the other hand, never did. I always wanted to hear him tell me he loved me, but he never did. If I recall correctly, my dad never told any of us he loved us, but we knew deep inside he did.

As a child, sometimes I hated my daddy. He and my mother would argue. I never said a word, just cried inside when I would hear them argue.

I used to listen to him talk to my brothers about his life before he met my mother. He was cocky and mean, but we never knew why. We never knew why daddy was so mean. We just knew he was. Just remembering this about my dad today helps me be more compassionate toward others understanding their present behavior most likely derived from their past. Later, we learned my dad never knew his dad. He wanted to but was denied that right by my grandmother. As the years passed, bitterness toward my grandmother set in. He didn't become free until many years later.

As a child, I suffered from low self-esteem. My brothers teased me about my forehead and my dad taunted me about how skinny I was. He would say, "Girl, you going to grow up to be a schoolteacher."

I'd ask, "How do you know?"

And his response would be, "Because you are walking on pencils." Everyone except me would laugh.

Even though he made fun of me, he taught me a lot of useful skills: how to change a tire, lay sheet rock, paint a house, and more. I excelled at them all. Mother taught me to cook, clean, and handle money as young as ten years old. Like I said, I wasn't allowed to go to parties like my friends. It was always school, family, and church. What they called protecting me, I called restricting me. Mother was our neighborhood schoolteacher at Elm Grove school. I was in trouble often, but I excelled in my grades. I would get in trouble at school for fighting, bullying, and playing tricks on the teachers.

Since Mother taught me banking, daddy opened a bank account for me at fourteen years old. I worked with my mother at the dry cleaners she managed. Later I got cooking jobs on my own. I loved acting in production plays in my local school and repertory theater. I always said one day that I would become a millionaire from acting or modeling. Mother and daddy worked hard but never had much money. My parents instilled a good work ethic in me through the skills they taught me and the implementation of chores. I knew someday I would be the one to make us rich.

One day, my chore was to put out the garbage and I failed to do it because I felt it was my elder brother Jr's turn. If we talked back to our parents, our teeth would end up on the floor, but on that day, I had the nerve to argue when my dad asked me why I didn't put the garbage out. I can't tell you where my teeth ended up, but I can tell you he beat me so bad I never forgot it. Jr had to rescue me.

I was angrier than I'd ever been. For the first time, I accepted I needed the whippings I'd received prior because I was disobedient but that day, I was innocent. It was unfair. I hated him. Not long after that episode, I ran away from home to my sister, Jenell, in California. We'd been thick as thieves since we were young. I dressed in my jeans with a silver glitter blouse and red apple cap. I forged my daddy's name, drew money of out the bank, and wrote a note to my brothers with instructions to take care of Mother.

It was the summer of 1973. I got a cab to the Gaslight Motel in Gretna and stayed until my friend came to get me. He drove me to the bus station the next morning. A one-way ticket to California was $87. I'd never ridden a bus alone or gone anywhere for any distance by myself.

A man sat beside me at the back of the bus who talked all the way from New Orleans to San Antonio where we changed buses.

I told him I was running away to California. He knew I was alone.

I got off the bus to watch the drivers transfer the luggage to the other bus, calling the names as they went. They called everyone's name except mine. I inquired about my luggage to no avail. Two of my bags were gone. The man that sat beside me was gone too.

I told the bus driver, who told the police, and that's when the confusion began. No one spoke English around me except the bus driver and most of the passengers. I started to cry when the officer asked me for identification. They proceeded to call authorities about a missing child.

It was about a two-hour layover because of me, and they never found my luggage. I called my mother, and I could hear the fear and despair in her voice. She knew I left because I hated my dad. She gave the phone to my dad but I didn't say a word. I just listened to him tell me to come home.

I didn't go home. Eventually, I arrived at the Long Beach bus station where my sister came to pick me up. We hadn't seen each other since we played church at my aunt's house.

Janell was what all the guys called "fine". And on top of that, the girl could sing. Some days we would sit around and sing oldies the whole day. "Oh, What a Night" by the Dells, "Sitting on the Dock of the Bay" by

Otis Redding, and "Just my Imagination" by The Temptations. All day long we would sing.

The first thing I did was get a job before school started and get in church. I joined St Luke Baptist church where my sister attended and never missed going because that's what I knew. I joined the choir and often sang solos. The preacher, Reverend Chin, called me "Precious Lord" and would often call me to sing the song "Precious Lord" before he would get up to preach.

I began working at a convalescent hospital in Long Beach for $1.90 per hour. All I could see were bright lights and big city. I was at the hospital temporarily and was going to do whatever it took to fulfill my dreams. My best friend at work was Shelly. She had a beautiful daughter with cerebral palsy. I often wonder if she's still alive today.

Shelly worked the streets and the hospital to take care of her daughter. When she first told me, she worked the streets, I freaked out. I felt like I was on a Hollywood set. But it wasn't a set, it was real. She told me how I could even make $100-$500 a night depending on how much I did.

"You don't think I'm going to work no streets? You mean as a prostitute?" I asked.

"No, silly. Just deal with the rich freaks. All they want you to do is whip them with wet towels, urinate in their mouths, make them cry, and they'll pay you $100. Most times they're stoned on cocaine. You'll be done sometimes less than fifteen minutes. Sometimes Shelly would make in one night what it took us to earn in a month at the hospital."

My mouth hung open, probably like yours is right now. I thought to myself, "You've got to be kidding me! Man, I can't do that! My mother would kill me, and my daddy would kill me twice." I thought about it a few weeks. The more of Shelly's money I saw, the more I wanted to do it.

After some serious thought I decided to do it. Shelly gave me her corner to work along with clear instructions on what to look for and told me to be there at 10pm. Do you believe I had the nerve to pray for protection? In my mind I could see God shaking his head.

I was getting dressed, scared to death, shaking, and pacing back and forth in the house. I dared not tell my sister. I was shaking so bad, I lit a joint, chickened out, and went to bed. The phone rang. We didn't have voicemail back then, so the phone kept ringing until I woke up. It must have been ringing a long time because, when I answered, Shelly was screaming and crying hysterically.

"Oh, thank God! thank God!" I asked what that was about. I thought she would be angry because I didn't go.

"Did you hear the news?"

"No. I've been asleep." Shelly burst into tears again.

Her words were "There was a girl working that same area I sent you to, and I thought it was you. She was found in the trunk of a car strangled with her panty hose. She wasn't raped, but she was strangled, and I thought it was you."

I sighed a deep breath. Lord, have mercy. Seems like God protected me even during the dumbest decision I could have ever made. Guess He did answer my prayer.

During my time in California, I was introduced to more than marijuana, which I'd already made my acquaintance with back at home: Angel dust, cocaine, heroin, black mollies, valium and more. If you didn't do any of those, you needed to graduate. I thought to myself, "This is not where I'm supposed to be."

School was about to begin. Folks at home had already said I would probably get pregnant and quit. Me? Pregnant! Now that was a joke. I was almost eighteen and still a virgin. If they said I wasn't gonna finish school, I was going to finish for sure and nothing was going to stop me. I got that attitude from my daddy.

I decided to go to a school called Leewood, which was about to be integrated at the time. I didn't know much about anything in Leewood, but I was told racism was evident there, including in the schools. They didn't lie about that one. It was about 20% black. The first week blacks were there, some of the students draped toilet paper over the school campus and racial writings appeared everywhere. No niggas allowed. The story was that boys who did this weren't even students at Leewood.

Nevertheless, it resulted in a riot. The fights were on. The police were in on it. It wasn't a pleasant sight. Somewhere in the mix, I was hit in my stomach by a cop. The uproar may have lasted less than a week. I only attended Leewood for 1 year and returned to Louisiana to graduate.

Before leaving California I did what I never thought I would: I lost my virginity to a married man. I felt like a dog, empty and alone. I'd given away something that only the man I would live in holy matrimony with for the rest of my life deserved. I cried for months.

When I returned home, I begged my dad's forgiveness for rebelling and leaving the way I had. We became very close after that, and our relationship was authentic. I didn't know it at the time but, instead of being happy about the restoration of my relationship with my father, my mother became insecure. She accused me of loving my dad more than her.

Here it goes again, Lord. WHY?

After graduating high school in New Orleans, my parents didn't want me to return to California. But they supported and gave me their blessings anyway.

In May 1975, I graduated and returned to California.

I attended Long Beach City College on the Pacific Coast Highway. In college, I was introduced to everything I had seen on TV: drugs, adultery, fornication, manipulation, fighting, scamming, and never-ending partying. I didn't like smoking marijuana because it made me sleepy, but I did it so I could be accepted. My choice of drug became cocaine because it made me feel confident and bold in my time of weakness and fear.

I made my way to Hollywood and enrolled in Wiest Barron Hill School of Television because of my love for acting. A new agent referred me to a photographer named Victor. I met with him on three occasions for facial modeling photos. The first two sets were good. On the third set, I was changing into a bathing suit when he called me out before I was finished. He sat on a barstool and pulled me toward him with great strength. He told me to remove the bathing suit. I was shaking, asking him why. My heart was beating so fast and the tears were rolling down my face.

He said "If you scream, I will hurt you real bad. And if you tell anyone, I will use these pictures inappropriately." He forced me to sit on him on the barstool.

All I remember were silent tears. I know what it means to suffer in silence. Again. Why?

I fell further into darkness when I faked a surgery on my feet: an insurance scam. I was introduced to an insurance man from Los Angeles who assisted me in this unsuccessful scamming endeavor. Afterwards, he became my husband and we moved to Long Beach. It was there that we met Sharon and Stud, our new best friends. All we did was smoked pot, snort cocaine, and party. It's funny how we still ended up in church every Sunday. My life spiraled downward. With the cycle of partying and the hollow routine of church, I became even more discontented and empty.

I prayed a lot, but something was still missing. My elder brother, Jr, sent us a book called "Religious but Lost" by L.R. Shelton. I was offended, but my husband, Harry, read it diligently. He was ready to move to New Orleans to learn more, but I wasn't. The book describes how people can be in church all their lives, singing in the choir, serving in every ministry faithfully, living what the average person would call a good life, and still die and go to hell. I knew I was in church faithfully because that's how I grew up, but I was still disturbed by the message. Why would a loving God send me to hell? At that time, I didn't know that God doesn't send anyone to hell. It was my own unbelief that would send me to hell. The very thought of this tormented me.

It was Harry's desire for us to move back to New Orleans, so in 1979, we arrived in a little town called Harvey where my parents lived on the west bank of the Mississippi River. It was the same house I grew up in ever since I was six years old. My parents loved Harry like their own. My brothers initiated him by beating him up and turning him upside down in our yard until my mother yelled, "Let that boy alone, y'all." They called it fun, but Mother wasn't pleased with the way they welcomed him.

Regardless, it was a happy day when we moved back home. Harry wanted to get out of California, which was where he'd been all his life. We had a few challenges with some of his family, so he was ready. I'd vowed I would never return to Louisiana to live so I wasn't ready at all. But I went because Harry wanted to. Reading Pastor Shelton's book prompted us to make the decision.

Harry was a special gift to my dad because of his love for construction and his desire to want to learn more. Though Daddy taught all his children the skill, no one was interested like Harry was. He was interested in what my dad did best: contracting.

Daddy stirred up the gift and nourished it in Harry. Harry became the best contractor on this side of the globe, in my opinion. At that time, I was searching for employment as well. I landed a position at Joe Ellen Smith Hospital and later received a certification as a medical unit secretary and entered nursing school. God's blessings poured upon us. My brother began showing me in the word of God, how much God loves me, how God had forgiven me from my sins by sending His Son Jesus to die in my place, and how He was just waiting for me to receive that. I couldn't shake this. I thought I knew it already, but it was different. It was like a new awareness.

My husband and I joined a church in Algiers, not far from where we lived. There weren't many blacks, and the pastor was obviously prejudiced. Pastor Green would never look me in the eyes when speaking to me and addressed Afro-Americans from the pulpit as "you people." Sometimes we would come together with a few friends and study God's word on Saturdays or when we ate dinner. Others would drop by to join us.

My brother was quite knowledgeable in some areas of God's word and many flocked to hear him teach. The pastor became jealous and told my brother to go preach somewhere else. Later, my brother introduced us to a black couple, Jalisa and Al. They were the sweetest couple, and we became very close.

They spoke of how much they loved Jesus and I wanted that badly. My life had been spiraling downward and became empty. Going to church meant nothing anymore. I was just going through the motions and feeling thirsty for more. Jalisa and Al spoke of trusting God and relying on him for simple life situations. I wanted that kind of confidence in God. They talked about how much God loved them. Of course, I couldn't imagine someone loving me that way and being that certain about it.

I wanted what they had. I wanted a relationship with Jesus like that. And I was convinced I needed one.

The greatest story that will ever be told from my life is how and when I received Jesus Christ as my Lord and Savior and the new perspective of my life in Him. I had no idea that the sinful life I once lived had come to an end and my new life, my new identity and faith, had just begun.

The more I read the Bible, the more I understood I needed forgiveness. Suddenly, it made sense. It didn't matter that I was raised in the church, sang in the choir, had Christian parents, or did good deeds. The Bible said man's righteousness in God's eyesight was as a filthy rag (Isaiah 64:6). Good Lord, that's heavy. I understood the bad news was that I was a sinner, that God requires perfection. Surely no one was perfect, certainly not me. Either I was going to accept God's payment for my sins or pay for them myself. The bible says the payment for sin is death (Romans 6:23).

I didn't want to die or remain separated from God. I get it now. It was about repenting of my sins and receiving God's perfect payment, His son, Jesus (John 1:12). The story of the woman at the well paralleled my life in an eerily familiar way. Jesus tells her to "go and sin no more" after living a sensual life. She doesn't fight the exposure. She believes He is Jesus Christ, Son of the living God. As a result, she heralds His name throughout the city. "Come see a man who told me all about myself"(John 4:29).

As I read that verse, it became real to me. It is only by grace that I'm forgiven and saved through faith, something I cannot see but am able to receive. This is a gift from God and there's nothing I can do to earn it. "My God! My God! Please forgive me," I cried out. "I believe that I'm a sinner, and I accept your love for me. Thank you for saving me. How could I have waited this long to experience your love for me?"

I could almost hear God say, "I found you alone a long time ago. I was waiting for you to receive my love by faith. Just faith, believing I gave my only Son to die in your place. He is the only perfect one, the only sinless sacrifice." There is nothing that I could have done to earn this gift of eternal life.

I accepted that God loved me from the beginning. My heart cried tears of joy knowing I had a direct connection with Him through prayer. I understood God was my heavenly father and desired communication with me. Just as I would ask my earthly father for guidance, I could go to God just the same. We began trusting Christ as Lord and Savior of our lives and we turned to God, asking for help in receiving the one thing we wanted more in life: children.

Harry wanted twelve children, but I wanted two. Since the doctors said I would probably never be able to have children or never carry a normal pregnancy and give birth, we called God out on the table. We prayed that God would open my womb like he did for Hannah (Samuel 1:19) and Sarah (Genesis 21:2).

We saw doctor after doctor to no avail. Why Lord, why? My heart broke more with every miscarriage. We were committed to trusting God to honor His word. We knew it was God's will for us to get pregnant so we prayed God's will. "And this is the confidence we had in coming to God: that if we asked anything according to his will, he heard us. If we know he hears us, whatever we ask, we know we have the petitions we desire of him "(1 John 5:14-15). We never gave up. Five years later we were blessed with a beautiful baby boy.

After so many years of struggling and twelve hard hours of labor, Harry Jr arrived. I wept tears of joy and thanked God over and over as I held my son in my arms and stroked his little tiny face. What an amazing Father we serve. We brought Harry Jr home and dedicated him back to God. My daddy lifted Harry Jr up toward heaven and thanked God, asking God to use him for His glory.

At that time, we were still going to the church in Algiers. The bible classes my brother taught were getting packed with more Caucasian brothers and sisters than ever. On one Sunday, the pastor's jealousy of my brother's popularity kicked in. He shouted from the pulpit, "You people need to go back to Africa where you came from!"

As a new Christian, I was "one step from stupid" as the saying goes. That was the day I realized God saved my soul and not my flesh. My temper wasn't gone anywhere. There was no deliverance in that area of my life. I stood up to answer him, primed for a fight, itching to release the anger I'd bottled up and forgotten. I could hear my brother saying, "Bay Sista sit down!"

I was a new Christian and had been taught the three stages of salvation. The lesson I learned that day was that positional salvation was immediate. The moment I believed in the Lord Jesus Christ by faith, I was saved from the penalty of sin. In other words, the sins that I committed past, present, and future have been paid for by Christ alone.

When God looks at me, He sees His Son who knew no sin. According to Ephesians 2:8-9, "it is by grace that I am saved through faith", not anything that I have done to earn it. It's simply a gift of God, so I can take no credit for it.

I understood that day that my flesh was not saved, and it was evident by my own behavior. I was able to see I switched places with Jesus upon confession of my faith in Him, God's Son. Instead of giving into my anger, I sat down when my brother spoke. I learned practical salvation, or sanctification, is a process of growth and I hadn't grown one inch when it came to my anger. These types of episodes kept happening so eventually we left the church and began studying God's word at home, praying for direction.

CHAPTER 3

IT LOOKED LIKE A CHURCH TO ME

What appeared to be a simple Bible class was a cult in seed form. The preacher, Tom, was young and could recite much of the King James version of the Bible verbatim by memory. His eyes would focus laser sharp on yours, unblinking, like he was staring straight through to your soul. His opening phrase was always, "Beloved, how are you doing?"

We were excited about the invitation to attend that Bible class across the river since we were looking for a new church. The first thing I noticed was how large the families were that attended the class, the vast number of children had. That alone frightened me to death. God answered our prayer with one child, and I was content with that. We felt an overwhelming pressure that a large family would be expected of us.

The couples were kind to us, but the conditions were poor. I sat down on the sofa and sunk all the way to the floor. My husband pointed at the rodents, disgusted by the squalor.

I'd never heard a man preach like Tom before. He was a teacher preacher and his knowledge of the Word of God captivated you in a strange way. He taught for hours. We would sing songs from scriptures in the Bible. Each person would make their own melody. The words were straight from the Bible, but the melodies were unique.

We felt reluctant and skeptical about the preacher and his church. Our friends, Jalisa and Al, joined us and their feelings were mutual. Something was off about that place. What startled us the most was that people served

Tom like he was a king. He justified their service to him with passages of scripture. "Obey your leaders and submit to them" (Hebrews 13:17). "Whoever rebels against the authority is rebelling against what God has instituted" (Romans 13:2). "Let the elders that rule be counted worthy of double honor, especially those who work hard at preaching and teaching" (1 Tim 5:17).

Of course, I was a young Christian, newly born into the faith and had no clue the Word of God gave warnings of this type of deception. In Ephesians 4, Paul gives us a clear description of God's goal through church leadership and mature believers. Throughout that

chapter you find the primary goal of the church is to mature and perfect the saints for edifying of the body of Christ so that we (the body of Christ, the believers) will no longer be tossed back and forth by every wind of doctrine, by the trickery of men, and the cunning craftiness of deceitful game. Another translation states that God wants us to develop so we can mature younger

Christians, making them a harder target for imposters. They're out there and that's where Harry and I landed.

Tom took every leadership scripture out of context to justify his own intentions. What freaked me out the most was that I hadn't shared any of my life with him but spoke to me as if he knew my whole life story. As a baby Christian I thought he had superpowers. Today, I'm able to do the same thing if I talk to a person long enough. It was merely discernment by the power of the Holy Spirit which is available to every believer.

The so-called leadership were all women, three sisters. They were all welcoming and cordial in the beginning, but the pastor often called me rebellious and instructed the middle sister to scorn me. It was obvious she obeyed against her will. The older one had no problem cutting people up and breaking spirits. The men that were there were inferior and subordinate. But again, WHY Lord?

CHAPTER 4

WHAT DID I LEARN WHILE THERE?

Even in the midst of this madness, God was up to something. I was aware of the selfish person I used to be but had the desire to become a more giving and compassionate person. Pastor Tom knew I suffered from insecurity in so many ways after I shared my life story, and he used that knowledge to manipulate me. He would tell me, "You are fearfully and wonderfully made." Then he would remind me of when I was taking drugs and living sensually; if I didn't submit to him, I would return to that way of life. Deep inside I knew I wouldn't, but he was rather convincing. He often reminded me that my goal was to become like his leaders.

He would ask, "Beloved, you know Pastor cares about your soul?" and show me scripture: "Obey them that have the rule over you for they watch for your souls as those who will give an account." (Hebrews 13:17). Tom would say, "God wants you to be obedient." Today, as I think about it, I can see so clearly what Paul meant in Ephesian 4:11-16, how skillful some people can be in their deceit. All these passages were true, but he used them to control people. It was demonic and crazy. He knew I wanted to please God as a young Christian, so he twisted the scriptures to his advantage, brainwashing and manipulating me. Because I have been there before, today I can spot it a mile away in churches, relationships, and people of power.

Tom's manipulation became more evident when he assigned my husband and I to serve another couple and their four children. The wife's name was Loren. I'm not sure how long she had attended Tom's church, but he had total control of her family and marriage. She and

54

her husband were separated. The pastor even told her when she could be intimate with her husband. When her last child was conceived, she wept because she really didn't want to go. I didn't know what to do. I couldn't say anything to anyone for fear I would bring harm to her.

I wondered how she could be so submissive, yet I was headed down the same path, unaware. Loren and I formed a deeper connection when I taught her how to bake. We became best friends, more than the leadership intended. She shared her fears with me, and I vowed to keep them. Loren had an illness she was supposed to have died from some years prior. The pastor convinced her that the reason she lived was because of her commitment to him and his ministry.

Although his abuse was appalling, Tom taught me some valuable lessons, such as the power of meditation on God's word. He said if I wanted to have control over my body and not sin against God with it, I should meditate on God's word. If meditating on God's word would make me free, I was going to do it. Together my husband and I began to memorize God's word beginning with 1 Corinthians 13. As we did this together, our relationship heightened. We laid the foundation of God's love for our children as we taught them the power of having God's word in their hearts as well. We never went to bed angry, we flourished in business, and I became less selfish.

But I became more submissive to Tom which led to more manipulation. It wasn't long before the leader began asking questions about our marriage and our sex life. He would ask if my husband was gentle. Since my husband always wanted twelve children, this subject piqued his interest.

The pastor would say to me, "Don't you want to honor God and be a good wife to your husband?" Of course, my answer was yes, but I really didn't want any more children. I stopped taking birth control pills well before Harry Jr was born and was using natural family planning (NFP) for birth control quite well. When the leader convinced us of God's will for me to populate, we dropped NFP and ended up with four more sons. That man was so cunning. Brainwashing was an understatement.

Tom believed in excommunication, which is biblical. But he excommunicated anyone that disagreed with him or the leaders which is not biblical. My husband was excommunicated when he refused to acknowledge someone's gift or task in leadership. When he admitted his error, what the leadership called repentance, he was allowed to return.

Only certain people were able to access what Tom called the "meat of God's word." He used Hebrews 5:13 totally out of context, calling all of us babes in Christ because we didn't have access to this special "meat" of God's word. He was the only one that could give it to us.

You were considered spiritually stronger than everyone else if you had it.

Everyone walked on eggshells for fear of saying something wrong and being excommunicated. My brother and husband were dismissed, excommunicated from the church, leaving me there with my children.

CHAPTER 5

THE TRAP OF FEAR

The fear that caused me to feel trapped was not a fantasy. One might ask, "Why didn't you leave with your husband?" During that time my husband became quite passive aggressive in many ways. There was no question whether Harry and I loved each other, we were just two young believers caught up in a web of Satanic forces without an escape.

The pastor told me I had to leave my husband, stating that he had strayed from God. I never knew until recently that my husband was dismissed because he asked, "Didn't the Bible say that man has to take care of his own family and the wife is to be submissive to her husband and not another man?" That's when the pastor put him out. I never knew why, and my husband never told me.

There were a few families with children that were being disobedient toward their parents, just as I did at that age. They were all males and Tom told us they would soon die because of it, and they did. He didn't state the type of death they would experience, but he told everyone to expect them to die.

One young man went into the military and was killed after he came home. Tom called his death prior to that.

By then, everyone including me were on pins and needles. No one trusted anyone. I was scared to death.

By the last time Harry was excommunicated, I was so scared I was going to do whatever Tom told me. I left my husband as instructed and moved to a double house in the Treme area of New Orleans. My oldest child was nine and my baby was almost two. I started a job as a caretaker for a ninety-six-year-old woman. I cooked for her and sat there to make sure she didn't leave. She was an Alzheimer's patient who thought it was still the time of slavery time. "Scrub those floors," she would yell out, but I'd just sit there and write.

I wanted to go home so badly. Every time I heard a knock at the door, I jumped. Whenever the phone would ring, my heart would race. The school year was almost over when my two older children saw their dad working in the area. I prayed so hard. God answered. I was reading and I ask God to show me the right path. It was a silent time in my life. I kept thinking, "He called those deaths." Everybody was frightened to death.

I'd been gone for an entire school term of eight months when he called my husband's death. But why? My husband was no longer there. That was the last straw. The Holy Spirit led me to Colossians 2:6-23.

Paul reminds the Colossians that Jesus Christ is Lord, and He is the one to follow. They had been saved from under the law and were now under grace. They were freed from legalism and encouraged not to return. He tells them not to let anyone condemn them for what you eat, drink, or celebrate. He tells the Colossians not to let anyone condemn them by insisting on pious self-denial.

Do this, do that, touch not, taste not. I was able to see that was where Satan had used Tom in my life. He was teaching salvation by faith plus Tom's rules. God showed me I had more fear of Tom than I did Him. God showed me I had placed a man where only God belonged. I called my husband and my parents and I went home.

CHAPTER 6

REUNITED BUT BROKEN

I didn't know how my husband would respond; all I knew was that I was going home.

I called it my escape. I was going home to my husband after being separated for an entire school term.

The process of forgiveness wasn't easy for either of us. Though happy to see each other, we were both angry and bitter. I wanted nothing to do with anyone who professed Christianity and I didn't want to go to anyone's church. Harry said he had been out of the church a while as well. He was angry because I left him upon instruction of Tom. But we united with our families and started attending reunions and gatherings again. I was back to serving my husband, which was my joy. Breakfast, lunch, and dinner were ready just as I had learned from my mother. My heart filled at the sight of him eating like he missed it.

I knew I loved God and He loved me. I was so wounded by those who called themselves Christians and didn't want to be anything like them. As far as I was concerned, they were phony. I just wanted Jesus. We visited churches where my family would sing, but I wouldn't open myself up to the pain of relationships again. At times, singing brought me comfort but writing soothed me more.

All five of my boys would sing "Falling in Love With Him" by Lanny Wolfe.

They would sing that everywhere, reminding me that I needed to be connected to a church family. The

Bible says don't forsake the assembling of yourself together …. (Hebrews 10:25 KJV).

Without community, there's no growth. Community consists of people and people bring challenges. Where no challenge exists, no growth exists. My knowledge of God's word clashed with my faith because I really wanted to be alone. I'd spent seven years in that cult calling itself a church memorizing books of the Bible. For the first time, I was obeying the Bible because I wanted to, obeying God because I wanted to. I was obeying God because I loved Him and not because a man told me to. I felt freedom like never before. Because I was free in Christ to do, be, or say anything I wanted to, it was about my choice being driven by love rather than fear: Love for God, my Heavenly Father.

Just because God saved me by His grace, I'm forgiven. Should I continue to live in sin? Should I take God's grace for granted? The answer was clear. No. I shouldn't and I won't. The word I had hidden in my heart was real. According to Romans 6:12, I have the power to prevent sin from controlling me. I am no longer under the law but under grace.

As I was learning to embrace my faith again in a new way, the past I was putting behind me crept forward again. We heard on the news pastor Tom had been arrested for eight counts of child molestation. I don't know the details, but one young girl exposed him. Today, some of those girls are still suffering and badly damaged. Others are freeing females across the world with their testimonies. I had no knowledge of that indiscretion when I attended Tom's church and was thankful, he never approached me in that way. I thought of what I went through as a teenager. If he'd approached me, he may not have lived to tell it. Back then, I wasn't as strong or free as I am today.

CHAPTER 7

SICK UNTO DEATH?

After being given six months to live, it was time to put the word of God, I'd spent seven years memorizing to the test. Does it work?

I hadn't taken medicine of any kind for seven years because the cult didn't allow it. It was without balance because God blessed us with doctors. Luke was a doctor (Colossians 4:14). I suffered greatly, losing muscle strength, and experiencing weakness. At times, I couldn't pick up a coffee cup. Once they even said it was lupus. I was scared, in pain. My parents and brother were a wreck as I went through test after test with no conclusive results. After a year, I finally had an answer.

My sed rate(erythrocyte sedimentation) was extremely elevated, revealing a high amount of inflammation in my body. My CPK was horrible as well: That determines the amount of stress the muscles are in and helps to ascertain tissue damage. They diagnosed me with polymyositis which they said was controllable with medicine. I shared the news with my husband and parents. My husband said nothing. It was as if I didn't exist. My parents were frantic and in unbelief.

Four doctors came to tell me if I didn't take the medicine they proposed, I wouldn't live another six months because of muscle weakness to the lungs and heart. The thought of dying and leaving my children without a mother was devastating. Me, God? Why? I agreed to be treated with prednisone and, a few weeks after that, methotrexate.

The side effects were terrible. My head would spin, my heart would palpate fast for no reason, and I was short of breath. My weight shot up more than fifty pounds in three weeks. I frightened my children and myself. The only thing I remember my husband saying was "You don't look like you looked when I met you." My heart sank. Harry was never physically abusive, but his words were like daggers.

I didn't like the way I looked or felt because of the medicine so I prayed for days. My dad told me about Rev Malkmus who had a holistic remedy called the hallelujah diet. I attended the seminar he was speaking at in Metairie, LA. The point of his lecture was, "go back to the garden." Rev Malkmus was diagnosed with cancer at forty-two. When I met him, he was sixty-three. The man looked like plastic. His skin was so smooth, no wrinkles, and he was a quiet, spirited, articulate man. I remember he referenced Genesis 1:29. God made our bodies to heal themselves when given the proper nutrients.

If I took anything away from that seminar, I was going back to the garden. The hallelujah diet eliminates all processed and animal food and replaces them with organic raw plant-based foods.

Reverend Malkmus stated man lived 912 years before the flood and 110 years after the flood and after adding cooked food to their diet. It is said that there's no evidence of this. Many said he was a quack. I'm not sure about any of that.

All I knew was that I went to see him and with my diagnosis I had nothing to lose. My children had to help me drive my car. I drove with my elbow, and they would turn the steering wheel. Some days, I walked with a cane.

Harry was cold as ice during this time. He wouldn't help me turn-on a faucet to take a shower. I was devastated by his neglect but pushed forward for my children. I couldn't leave them without a mother.

Although my husband wasn't there for me, I was eternally grateful for my dad. He was healthy as an ox but supported me by making the lifestyle change with me. I juiced carrots, beets, mixed with barley powder. Seventy percent of my food was raw. Later, I added cooked veggies. I tapered myself off the prednisone even though the doctors told me not to. I took God's word at face value. The Bible says God's word will be "health to my navel and marrow to my bones" (Proverbs 3:8). All day long I would say this. I believed God's word.

It was a faith step, but in less than three months my weight dropped back to normal. I was able to lift my hands to walk a block without panting. No more head or heart spinning. After about eight months, I could stand up from a sitting position without assistance. My knees didn't bother me as much. Healing was mine. Every time I lifted my hands, praise came forth. My praise is real. I often heard my parents say, "You don't know God as a healer until you've been sick. "Now I understand. Today I work-out 3-5 days weekly. Thank you, Lord, thank you Father, for my praise.

CHAPTER 8

ROCKY ROAD

Divorce was the last word I ever thought would come from my lips. When I met Harry, I was twenty. He was part of a bowling team and got me involved as well. I was never much of a bowler but because he liked it, I joined him. Bowling was his life outside of work. With my illness, it was difficult for me to be around smoke, and the alleys were always cloudy. I never mistrusted him or suspected anything.

One morning, the boys went to work with their dad and returned late evening. I asked, "How was your day?" They were upset.

They said "Daddy left us outside playing all day while he was in the room with Ms..."

My jaw dropped, but I didn't say anything. Harry told me he was friends with a lady that attended the same church he did when I was gone for those eight months. That's whose home he was working at.

We allowed Harry Jr to work with another one of Harry's friends. He came home one evening and said, "Mama, Mr. Stone told me to give you Daddy's girlfriend's brake shoes for her car." That's when I started searching. I searched Harry's drawer one day and found a valentine's day card from the lady. Harry had moved out of our bedroom about two years after we were back together. I still prepared his meals, but we didn't have a physical relationship for an entire year unless I went up the stairs.

When we first married, we made a commitment to never leave the house without kissing each other even when we were mad. And even mad at each other, we kept that promise. So, he would come in from work, kiss me, warm his food, and up the stairs he would go. My illness flared up because of the emotional stress of rejection and I was unable to stay on track with my eating habits. My knees began to swell, weakness returned in certain parts of my body.

The phone rang, I answered and assumed it was a female client. I never felt insecure about him talking to women because of the nature of his business. But this time was different. I gave him the phone and sat at the foot of the stairs listening to him telling the woman he was tired of me being sick. I sat there listening quietly for a long time as my suspicions were confirmed. My faith wasn't as it is today. A battle raged inside of me. I wanted to physically harm him, but I knew I should settle for divorce.

He leaned against our bedroom dresser as we talked. I told him I wanted a divorce because of the way he treated me and his cheating. He didn't deny it. He didn't hesitate to answer me. He said, "Ok." I think I was more devastated that he didn't deny it.

He calmly packed a few things and left without any remorse or putting up a fight. It was like he'd been waiting for that day long before I asked. In the beginning, he would pick up the boys to go bowling with him and a woman would be in the front seat of the car. It wrecked me to see him with another woman and watch how badly it affected my boys. The oldest was acting out in school.

Our divorce was final in 1998. I felt myself being angry with God for my choosing to serve him, to live a life of purity and not getting the same in return from my husband. Those thoughts came from the pain. God had delivered me from a life of promiscuity, and I never wanted to go back there again. When I became a Christian, I vowed to God not to be unfaithful to my husband. It's better not to make a vow to God than make a vow and not keep it (Ecclesiastes 5:4-6). He takes no pleasure in that. Not only did I want to keep my vow to God, but I wanted to be faithful to my husband and myself.

I even asked God to kill me if I sinned against him in this way. That's how much I despised my own sin. My heart was broken beyond repair, the pain was worse than any I had ever experienced before. We had been together for nearly twenty-one years, married nineteen of them. This was the man I thought I'd spend the rest of my life with. I thought since we were out of the cult that nothing and no one could ever tear us apart. I had no idea about the secret strategies of Satan in a believer's life.

Satan's objective is to kill, steal, and destroy. Though I read the bible repeatedly, I wasn't able to fight. I had a sword in my hand but was unable to lift it for battle. I had the buckler surrounding me, yet my entire body was exposed to danger. Little did I know, Satan was using the weapon of unforgiveness with both of us. It confirmed that having knowledge is useless without the power to apply it.

Although I struggled daily to get past my heartache, I had more important matters to attend to. I knew I should return to school, but I needed to do something quick. Just the thought of being a statistic on governmental assistance made me sick to my stomach. I realized every person's situation is different. Every person's outcome is different, but this was not going to be me. I had seen it all around me and I wasn't going to do that even if that meant having two jobs scrubbing floors.

I went into survival mode. It was all about my children. Their father paid child support, but it wasn't nearly enough. I had to find something steady and lucrative. After graduating from NEC through SUNO as a medical assistant, I completed an internship program at the parish prison. The work was steady, but not as lucrative as I needed it to be. I united myself with a well-known church in the city. Although I kept myself separated and was afraid to build relationships, I attended Bible classes faithfully.

What impressed me most about my new pastor was that he was transparent about his life. When he taught, he applied his lessons to personal experience, so his parishioners felt connected to him. My soul was fed there ,but to be closer to home I began attending a small church on the west bank. That's where I really began to see God's love and understand this spiritual journey I was on.

I began healing from my divorce through my faith but the emotional stain on my children remained. They looked forward to spending time with their father but experienced many broken promises. I tried to make up for that by allowing their friends to come over on Sundays. There was fun and basketball with the boys in the neighborhood. But nothing outweighed those packed bags returning from outside after another broken promise. My dad and brothers were by my side through the struggle. I'd have to leave for work and one of them would handle breakfast and get the boys off to school.

Because I was away from my sons often, I figured I needed a school system to water the same biblical foundation principles we had already laid. Deep in my gut I felt private school was the answer at that time. I was financially blessed enough to enroll the two oldest and the baby in private school.

With that burden off my shoulders, I gave myself over to mastering my skills at the prison. One day a friend asked me if I'd like to earn a whole week's worth of pay in less than ten minutes. Of course, I wondered if it was legal. I'd heard these same words in my wilder days, and I was always open to more opportunities and more cash. He reintroduced me to my passion for networking in a prominent legal company. I quit the prison and began to travel, taking my boys with me to every event. In less than six weeks I earned $12,000. The financial burden was lifting. However, our fatherless home became more of a challenge as the boys got older.

Harry Jr was a loner but excelled in school. After the Columbine shooting in Colorado, most schools were cautious. My son made a bogus threat to blow up the school and was expelled from all Jefferson Parish schools. He left home.

After that, my second son, Brian, became a surrogate husband. Now he was the oldest male in the house. Wherever I went, he always wanted to come. My parents called him an "old soul" because he always wanted to be around older people. I dumped my frustration, pain, and bitterness upon him as a child, never considering him being only 12 years old whether it would affect his relationships an adult. My middle child was Kenneth. He was unintentionally ignored because he was the middle child. But he was the one who made the family laugh with his silliness even in the midst of sadness. He didn't want to attend private school, so I

81

didn't force him. I told him what my parents told me, "Whatever you want to become, be the best of it."

My fourth son, Pete, was a task-oriented child who would accomplish what most children couldn't. He loved a challenge and couldn't wait to prove you wrong just like his grandpa. Anything that was broken, he fixed. Tyler was my fifth son and never experienced the absence of a father until he was old enough to realize it. His father left when he was four and my dad and brothers were always there for him. Tyler went to live with his dad around age fourteen.

Although the struggles at home with my children continued for many years, I made great strides with my work. I dropped my contract with the legal company when they experienced some difficulties. I told myself I would never go back to a regular job because I enjoyed the freedom I had there. But I ended up landing a job at a major funeral home in the city. I made an exception because they allowed me the same freedom. The first year

I was there I achieved "rookie of the year" for getting $100k volume in sales and won a trip to San Destin, Florida.

I loved sales because I loved serving people. Shortly after that I became a licensed insurance professional for the state of Louisiana. Two years later, I was invited to assist in building a company in Alabama because of my networking skills. That company dissolved but a group of us started our own trading company. It was there that I gained confidence in training others. My friends were people that thought like me and my relationships expanded across the United States. I became a national trainer for the company and my dad traveled with me to the larger events.

I loved traveling with my dad for work, but in 2004 things took at bad turn. My daddy had his annual checkup and was convinced to get intestinal polyps removed. It was supposed to be an easy, one-day surgery but it went south. The doctors clipped his intestines by mistake, and he became septic. On May 18, 2004, he passed away I was sick to my stomach. My boys were devasted. Our shock and sorrow cut deep at this sudden and tragic loss. I didn't know whether to blame God, I was so angry. My relationship with my dad as a child was rocky due to my own rebellion so my relationship was closer to my mother as a child. But for the last twenty-seven years of my life, my dad was my business partner and best friend. I just couldn't understand how God would take him. He was never sick. I just couldn't understand this sudden loss.

In tears, questions flooded my thoughts. How could God take my dad? He was a servant, he was an honest man, he was a good husband, and an amazing father. He was my everything. How could this happen? He encouraged me. He believed in me. We had our differences, but our disagreements never lasted long. I talked to my dad every day of my life. I was his baby girl.

What were my boys going to do? What was I going to do? Again, Why?

I knew God would answer this question. I thought back to Romans 8:28. Do all things work together for my good?

I prayed, "I don't see the good in this, Lord. You have to answer this question." Four months later, my family experienced another devastating loss when my sister-in-law, my elder brother's wife, Mick, passed away. She suffered with lupus until God took her home.

Mick was my brother's pearl. They were married nine years. That woman was a heaven-sent angel for my brother. When she opened her mouth, her voice was soft, but her wisdom spoke volumes. She prayed and asked God to let her know when she was leaving and to give her the opportunity to say goodbye. He answered as requested and over 100 people came to the hospital to say goodbye. Our family was there by her side until she closed her eyes.

On top of all that, Pete's gregarious personality led him into acquaintance with the justice system. That year kept me on my knees for mercy.

On the brighter side, Brian decided to audition for a major reality talent show. He had our support as well as family and friends across the U.S. Everyone was so proud of him. The cast came to our church one Sunday morning after I cooked breakfast for them. He had the opportunity to fulfill one of his life dreams and off to Hollywood we went for the finale. Upon his return, he moved to Atlanta to continue his newfound career.

I purchased a Kia and was about to purchase my first home. By then, I was an independent insurance agent building my own agency through a Texas-based international marketing company. I was in love with helping people see the importance of protecting their families. That time I was building the agency I wanted, and the money was looking better than ever.

My best friend said, "Girl, you do nothing but work, serve people, and go to church." And she was right. She suggested I meet new people on a dating site. Although I promised myself, I wouldn't date or pray for a husband because I was terrified and wounded from the cult and the thought of another man having access to my children, I eventually decided to give it a shot.

That was scary for me, but I ended up meeting a lot of good people who became my friends. I met some crazies as well. There was one profile that attracted me. His profile read, "If you are looking for a booty call, please pass me by because Jesus is the Lord of my life."

Ever heard of "love at first sight"? This was "love at first read". His name was Taz, he lived in Texas and was a poet. Taz always had encouraging words for me. Although nothing came of it, we enjoyed each other's company. I looked forward to maybe meeting him one day.

CHAPTER 9

WHO SAID GOD DOESN'T MOVE IN A STORM

New Orleans is the place where anything goes. It's known for its around-the-clock nightlife and a vibrant cuisine that reflects its history. Nobody does the kitchen thing like "Nawlins". It's a good idea for tourists to lose ten pounds before arriving, because it's almost a guarantee they'll gain that much before they leave. Of course, we're most well-known for Mardi Gras, which is celebrated two weeks before Ash Wednesday.

It's a French term that means "Fat Tuesday". Mardi Gras is really the last day before lent, a forty-day period of fasting between Ash Wednesday and Easter recognized by Roman Catholics. When I was a child, we always celebrated Mardi Gras for the festivities. But now that I'm a Christian, I don't celebrate it anymore. It's a time when people overindulge themselves in whatever sinful behavior they want to before they begin their fast. It's celebrated with parades, alcohol, floats, and any sinful desire you can think of. Many tourists come to the Big Easy for the festivities. The other thing we're known for is our hurricanes.

The worst hurricane I remember as a kid was Hurricane Betsy in 1965. My dad brought us all into one room for about three days to wait out the storm. It was predicted the tree in our front yard would fall across the house, and it did. But we were safe. My dad made sure of it. The next bad one was Hurricane Camille in 1969. It didn't affect New Orleans as bad, but it damaged the Gulf Coast of Mississippi. Every year thereafter we experienced hurricane hype to evacuate until it fell on deaf ears.

Because of that disregard, people weren't moving fast enough when Katrina hit land. Governor Blanco called to all pastors over the news to encourage their people to leave the city. It was as clear that this storm was to make history. But many believed the news was crying wolf.

I was doing well financially, had purchased a new home, and was getting past being alone. I was just getting settled and didn't want to leave. Kenneth went to Houston with his girlfriend and her family. I thought we'd be back by the weekend, so we left home with only three days' worth of clothes packed. My elder brother called pleading with me to get my mother, handicap brother, and best friend and meet him at the Shell gas station early the following morning. The plan was to go to Shreveport to get a hotel, but the contraflow was horrible and there was no room. We drove until we hit the Texas state line. An eight-hour drive took us over sixteen hours.

In Texas, we still have nowhere to go. I had relatives I hadn't seen in over forty years that lived in Dallas, but I had no idea where they were. We ended up at a hotel in Tyler, Texas, a couple hours outside of Dallas, where they gouged us $800 for a three-day stay. Business owners took advantage of the evacuees. Gas prices soared. A pack of wieners were almost $8 at some corner stores.

We were safe inside the hotel watching the news. Over eighty percent of the city was underwater. It was over seventeen feet deep in some areas, over the roofs of houses. Some residents were waiting on roofs for help. I was thankful, confused, afraid, and frantic. I knew my baby was safe with his dad. Brian was already in Atlanta months before Katrina hit. Harry Jr and Pete lived together at the time, and I had no contact with them. They were the ones I was concerned about. I wasn't sure if they'd left New Orleans or not. All signals on cell phones were crossed. I prayed harder than I ever had before.

Somehow, we ended up at a Methodist church in Tyler, Texas, which was going through racial discrimination issues we weren't aware of at the time. They housed us in the gym with twin size cots and access to showers. They provided us with towels, food, and other necessities. For a week, we were the only ones there. Still no word from my two sons in New Orleans. I tried so hard to focus on the promises of God. My help is in the name of the Lord who made heaven and earth (Psalm 124:8).

I drowned my fear with the power of God's word. God you are my helper, you are with me (Psalm 54:4). We received word that a busload of evacuees was on its way to Tyler from New Orleans. I didn't want to be there when they arrived, so I prayed, and God answered. Many Texas families wanted to provide us housing individually but we didn't want to be separated. God showed up and blessed us with an apartment complex that had only been built six months earlier for students attending college. I retrieved my third child from Houston, and we had a three-bedroom apartment to live in.

God has a way of connecting dots we know nothing of. Guys from the dating site sent me cashier's checks and I was able to help my family. There was a church in Tyler that had a program to adopt a family in need of relief from Katrina. I made sure my whole family was adopted. After they were settled, it was time to work on me. God sent a dentist and his wife to knock on my door and ask what I needed. I thought to myself, "God, I know you're in control of my life, and this too has to get your permission." I told the dentist if he could get me a computer, I would be fine. I knew I could make money to provide for myself and my children.

The next day they brought me a new desktop computer, a kitchen table, two beds, and an iron. I wept, hugged them soundly, and thanked them more times than I could count. For over ten years I'd always been the one to give. And now someone gave to me. Katrina marked the beginning of the manifestation of 2 Corinthians 9:7-8 in my life. God truly moved in this storm, and I knew the best was yet to come. It says we should decide in our hearts to give. God loves a cheerful giver and God is able to make grace abound to me at all times.

I knew this because God's word said it but I acknowledged it through experience. God had been taking care of me all along, but the word of God came alive that day. A man once told me the word of God is like a diamond and, depending on the angle you turn it, you just might see a different cut. Yet, it's the same diamond, still bright, still shining, and still a diamond. I saw a different cut of diamond that day. I was so ashamed of my attitude toward the bus coming from New Orleans, I returned to the church to help with the evacuees.

My family would meet at the gym when all the families were eating dinner and we would sing praises to God who was our strength. The pastor of the Methodist church bonded with my brother and shared with him the racial issues the church was going through before we arrived. He was amazed at our faith in God, not knowing whether our homes were still standing or not. According to what we saw on TV, we assumed we were under water as well. But we were secure in the knowledge that God was providing for us and would continue to do so.

Two weeks after settling in, my middle child said he wanted to go live with his dad. He was eighteen when the storm hit, so my blessings went with him in tears. All my sons were gone, and it was time for me to sit in God's presence with no distractions to take care of others. That's what I was used to doing, and I loved it. Serving others was fulfilling.

After being in Tyler about thirty days, I got a call from Brian. He asked me to drive to Dallas to get his girlfriend because she needed a place to stay. I dropped everything and headed to get her. She lived with me for less than a year. To my surprise, before she left that young lady gave me flowers and words of appreciation for me and my love for God. I'm lost for words as I remember her departure. You never know who God is allowing to be encouraged by your life even in your struggles. Today, she has a heart for God and is dancing to his glory. As a mother, I think my son missed out on that one. But God's timing is perfect, and he knows exactly what he's doing.

I met some amazing people in Tyler, mainly the Hinton's. We united with their church, and it was during this time that I began to dig deeper into God's word. I was mournful about the fact my boys were grown and gone, but I had more time to study God's word in a way I hadn't before. Memorization wasn't a priority anymore, obedience was.

Image wasn't important, a genuine relationship with my heavenly Father took precedence over everything. But the more I searched the word, the angrier I became.

This Christian life is supposed to be better. Frankly, Lord, this is not what I envisioned. Have you ever felt that way? I thought, "Why me? Am I paying for sins I committed before I came to know Jesus? The ones after?" I needed to understand the despondent emotions I was feeling. Why was I raped? Why did I end up in a cult? Why didn't my marriage work? Why did I get sick? Why did my daddy die? It wasn't fair.

Why did I start projects and not finish them? Why did my boys grow up without a father? Why did I attend four colleges and only complete one? I cried out to God. I kept reading and trying to hear what he was saying. He didn't answer all of those questions at once, but he did reveal four things by His Spirit.

1. I was bitter inside myself.
2. I played the blame game, the victim.
3. I had never taken responsibility for anything.
4. God had given me freedom and the power to change all of this just by focusing on becoming a better me.

The answers to all these questions began with me, and the hardest thing in the world was to admit I was angry and bitter. It was time for me to take God at His word. I always thought I did, but really, I only did when it was convenient for me.

I was bitter toward my children's father. How could God let him live knowing he betrayed his promises by cheating on me? I wanted to see bad things happen to him. I didn't deserve to be treated the way he treated me. Every time I heard his voice, I cringed. All of this was going on inside me, but I never wronged him. I rejoiced whenever our sons realized he was a disappointment when he wouldn't keep his word. I never wanted them to hurt, but my pain and bitterness felt validated whenever Harry wronged others.

I blamed him for everything. If he hadn't suggested moving back to Louisiana, none of this would have happened. If he would have been less of a coward and stood up for me, we never would had fallen victim to that cult and weakened our marriage. He could have been angry with me all day long but why couldn't he stay connected with his sons? I blamed him for every bad relationship our sons had because he was the example. I blamed him for me getting sick.

God showed me where I should have been. He laid the blueprint out. It doesn't make much sense in the moment, but God has a plan. He's faithful to His own word even when we don't understand it. I remembered salvation in Jesus Christ was immediate. That was a done deal. I know I'm forgiven for my sins. However, sanctification, the act of being freed, is a process. The Colossians are encouraged to lead godly lives and our lives are hidden with Christ in God. This is a process according to Colossians 3:5. Mortify the sinful things that lurk inside of you (evil desires like blame, bitterness, sexual, and lust). To mortify is to slowly put something to death. It's a gradual process.

I wasn't free, I was still bound by my own sinful desires, feelings, and my past. I was in bondage to my own frame of reference. God gave me emotions but not so they could control me. Jesus told the disciples they were sanctified by "truth". The Word of God is truth John (17:17). So, the only way I could be freed of this was through the truth. I needed to take responsibility for my actions and not focus on the person that hurt me.

I knew I could have done better, but I wasn't about to take responsibility for any of it. Sometimes I would measure Harry's wrongness against mine. His offenses were greater than mine. That was pride in myself, and God hated it. God honors humility and it's through humility he will exalt us. Even when coming to

Christ, I had to take responsibility for my own actions and admit I was sinner, had sinned against a holy God, and acknowledge that I needed the salvation He gave through His Son. It was true daylight after a lifetime of darkness. I saw it and I cannot express the relief I experienced because of the person I saw. I didn't like it. The person I saw was ugly. The person I saw was unattractive, ill, and foul. The person I saw was me.

I'll never forget what my brother taught me. You can't change what you can't see but if you can see it, you can change it. I was ugly and I wanted to change it. The question was, what was I going to do about it? On my knees, I fell before God to forgive me.

I realized I had everything I needed to fix this according to 2 Peter 1:3. God has given me everything I need to live a godly life because of my relationship with Him. I repented before a holy God and changed my attitude immediately. I knew I was being influenced by Satan because he is an accuser of the brother. He comes to kill, steal, and destroy. Certainly, he had stolen my peace and was about to destroy my body. I realized my body would flare up in pain when I focused on the things that happened to me.

Lord, in the name of Jesus I'm so sorry for not only how I've treated others that hurt me, but how I've treated you. As I focus on how you've forgiven me, how merciful you are to me, how loving you are to me, how patient you are with me, the greater the shame I experience. That day my life changed. I wanted with every fiber in me to live peaceably with all people. The weight lifted from me was unexplainable. No one knew any of these struggles. Only God and my journal.

CHAPTER 10

TIME TO TEST IF YOU ARE REALLY

FREE

Six months after the city was reopened for contractors, Harry headed to New Orleans, leaving our baby son with his stepsister. We weren't on the best of terms, but in the midst of a hurricane and being displaced, at least we were communicating. I was facing what God had shown me about myself and the desire for answers from my husband.

I needed answers. They needed answers. All I could hear in my spirit was, "Guilty or not, fix you." That wasn't really the issue. What disturbed me most was that my child called saying he needed a haircut and that he was hungry. The anger rose inside of me like the Incredible Hulk, but by God's grace and amazing power I was able to restrain it. God's word is powerful in you when you apply it (Romans 6:12). Don't let sin reign or control you. Don't even give sin a vote in the way you conduct your life.

Moving to Dallas wasn't the plan. This was my first huge testing period after my revelation and deliverance. The same weekend Harry went back to New Orleans to start rebuilding, I packed my things, got a moving truck, and headed to Dallas. It was a difficult search, but I asked God to find me a place to live, and he provided. Tyler and I moved into a two-bedroom townhouse in Richardson. I was displeased with the government system during this time. People all around me who had never worked a day in their lives were receiving $10k-15k in government assistance. I was a beast and driven when it came to providing, but I only qualified for the initial $2,750. But once again, the mercy of God came through for me. He had supplied all my needs before, why would He not keep his promise again? I was beginning to get it. God had a track record with me. I was beginning to take Him at His word.

I hadn't held a 9-5 job in so long, but I was willing to do anything before me and be the best at it. I began working for a computer sales company. It was a new company and their call center consisted of only four people, including me. I knew this job wouldn't last too long because it was another low salary, third shift job. So, I continued my insurance business on the side to make up for the lost income.

The owner of the computer company was Jewish and God granted me favor with him. I became the sales trainer and night manager. I went after what I wanted and proposed a higher salary if he wanted me to train other employees. By God's grace, I built the call center from four representatives to 102 in less than a year. It wasn't long before I was earning $73k annually.

Since I'd found security and stability, next I needed to find a place of worship. There was a church directly across from where I lived, so I visited there on Wednesday nights for Bible class for about four months. It was a large church, which I wasn't into, but the pastor could really teach the word of God. His delivery was humorous, but he was transparent with his life experiences, so his lessons really stuck with me.

With my housing, job, and faith all on track, I decided it was time to reach out to friends once more. I remembered Taz, from the dating site, lived in Dallas. When I spoke with him, he had words of encouragement for me and wanted to know if I'd found a church home. My response was, "Not yet, I'm still looking, but I've been attending a church in North Dallas off Prestonwood."

He said, "Girl, that's the church I attend." Suddenly, I was excited to be uprooted by Katrina, to connect with someone I had been talking to for over a year. I was excited about the possibility of a new soulmate. The next Sunday morning, I could hardly wait until the pastor finished preaching. I felt someone pull my hair and say, "Hey, Marian."

We embraced each other. Although we didn't connect as soulmates, we greeted each other warmly for the next fifteen years. I believe he was the conduit God used to get me to that church. Today, he's married and doing well. Thanks, Taz, for allowing God to use you.

The mission pastor of my new church connected me with the ministry I loved so dearly: evangelism. With all my flaws, I knew undoubtedly that people needed Jesus and I had no problem teaching others to do the same as I had learned. The evangelism team was the lifeblood of the church. God called us all to be salt, light, and witnesses (Matthew 5:13-16). At my home church, my friends and I would share the gospel once a month about Jesus Christ coming to save sinners. For two years my dear friend and I used to go to the mall early Monday to tell people about Jesus. Folks thought they were going to the mall to shop, but they would end up submitting to Jesus. I used to get high on drugs, and now I get high sharing Jesus with sinners.

To my surprise and disappointment, there were only three guys carrying out the great commission. Why? There were two young men that loved God so dearly and they carried the torch of the great commission. The other one was impacting the kingdom for Jesus through an orphanage in Africa. I connected with them as well as a smaller church around the corner about sharing the gospel. I had been a praise and worship leader back home, but I had no desire to sing in anybody's choir. I only wanted to connect with a ministry group that loved sharing the love of Jesus Christ with others.

Around that time, Tyler graduated, and it was a rewarding day. God had freed me and placed a new song in my heart. I wanted the same thing for my sons. God blessed me to be able to accommodate my children's dad, his new wife, and our sons at Marriott Hotel across the street from my apartment. We hadn't been in each other's presence for a few years and the last time we were, there was tension in the air.

Shortly thereafter, I made an appointment to use my friend's home in New Orleans to have a family meeting. Growing up, the boys and I would have family meetings. This was the time I would allow them to say what was in their hearts, respectfully, and no one would get in trouble, good, bad, or indifferent. They were grown now and they needed a family meeting. The boys needed to deal with their bitterness and unforgiveness, and so did their dad. I couldn't give them the answers they needed to hear from their father. I wanted so badly for us all to be free. That day came and I journaled it afterwards. It was a challenge being the mediator and keeping the boys in order while giving their dad a chance to speak his heart. They asked questions, he answered.

Everyone had a chance to speak their minds. It ended with forgiveness and unstoppable tears.

From that day forward, Harry and I have had peaceful, open lines of communication. Sometimes he and his wife would come to Dallas to bowl and I would stop by to see them. Things began to happen and there was no doubt it was the hand of God. The doors started opening for me in Dallas. I became more confident. People sought me out for solving problems, though that's always been the case in my life.

I studied The Five Love Languages by Gary Chapman. It outlines five basic ways you can express or experience love with your partners. I used it when establishing every relationship I had. Since everyone is different and not everyone communicates love the same way, learning the five love languages helped to improve every relationship I developed once I discovered the other person's. I was able to give them what they needed.

A person feels more loved when their particular love language is expressed to them. You can possess more than one love language, but only one is dominant. I wasn't aware of this in times past. If I'm always expressing love in a language that isn't dominant to you, you may feel unloved by me. When communication is open between two people, exploring each other's needs can make the relationship more fulfilling.

CHAPTER 11

MORE BLESSINGS MORE TRIALS

Doors began opening for me to utilize the gifts God placed inside of me. I connected with Larry Moyer, Founder and President of Evantell Organization in Dallas, Texas and took his certification course. His program teaches born again believers how to share their faith confidently and clearly. His method was clear. It was ten words. Christ died for our sins and rose from the dead.

My ability to master and duplicate what I heard Larry do was a gift from God. I connected and bonded with his wife, and I followed her as she trained pregnancy resource center counselors how to share the gospel with the young girls that came for emotional and physical assistance. These girls were sometimes at their lowest in spirit, hungry, and thirsty. It was a great time to introduce the Savior who could feed them and give them water to never thirst again.

When a church in the area needed a trainer, our church sent me.

The Holy Spirit moved on the heart of my pastor, and he gave me the entire hour of his Bible class to share the importance of evangelism. I was so excited for an open door not only to exercise the gift God had given me, but to share with those that were eager to learn. Upon completing the hour, quite a few people expressed how it helped, while others expressed displeasure about the change in the pastor's format. Some even told me it wasn't the correct setting to do training.

For a moment, it hurt, but I knew what God had called me to do and I was confident and encouraged to press farther. The Pastor encouraged me to continue and said I had his support for the work of the ministry.

I also received an invitation from Pastor Michael, who was in charge of the missions department, to go to Africa to train pastors to teach their people how to share the gospel of Jesus. I was ecstatic! I didn't think about how I was going to get there. My confidence was in the Lord. At that point I believed if He opened this door, then He would surely provide. I spent a lot of time with Michael as he prepared me and five others for the trip. We learned some of the culture and a few phrases in an African language.

Because I was a networker and had no problem asking for what I needed, God touched the hearts of many people at the church, allowing me to raise $3500 in a very short period. The greatest thing I learned as a global missionary was the word flexible.

Often, plans change. Not daily, but sometimes momentarily. I've been told all my life that America is the greatest country in the world. In my opinion, I believe we are the most ungrateful people in the world, and we have more than most. On some of our trips we were allowed to bring items that would be helpful in their Christian growth as well as some personal items that may have been requested. I remember visiting a little village called Kafue. The families were so appreciative of a pair of socks or a pair of slippers. Sometimes they responded like I was handing them a million dollars. Sometimes leaving a tip equivalent to $3 in American dollars brought tears to a waitress' eyes.

My expertise is training and teaching believers how to share their faith. Many times, in America, when I would do these trainings. People would be hyped and excited in the moment. When I would see them a month later and ask them if they'd applied any of what they learned, more often than not, the answer was no with some excuse. When I was in South Africa training at the Nelson Mandela University, not only did the students learn but they applied it the same week. I trained pastors in Zambia. They expressed gratitude and shared how they applied it.

I was assigned the task of training another ministry in the church and the opposition became more evident. It was a ministry of over forty men. A few expressed how they didn't feel the training was for them because they weren't evangelists. This was heart breaking because they were professed and seasoned believers. I was shocked they weren't aware that all believers are called to be witnesses, salt, and light (1 Peter 3:15 Acts 1:8).

I was fine with disagreements, but I didn't do so well with attitudes. Every time the attitudes would arise, I would go through an inward battle as Paul described in Romans 7:21-25.

Can I be real with you, my reader? Yes, I love Jesus. He saved my soul but, not my flesh. These folks had no idea they were looking at the "grace of God walking." There were uncountable times when I wanted to lash out and beat up on someone. It was that person I once was trying to release. It was my old self. But I was reminded of who I was in Christ Jesus. Just because I was treated that way, I didn't have to respond to others the way I was treated.

I was finally getting that thing called, "die to self" (1 Peter 2:24 and Romans 6:1-6). When I read those verses, I was reminded I have the power to say no. My grandmother used to sing the hymn "Something Within" by Lucie Eddie Campbell.

They called it "something," however I know today it was God's Holy Spirit. I held that "something" within me through my struggles with many of the congregation members. I believe God rewarded me with Hector and

Alma who had ministered for over thirty years at a prison in Oklahoma.

They invited me to join them every first Saturday of the month. I did an evangelism training several times, and participated in witnessing to inmates during annual revivals. Every month, I would minister in song. Hector was one of the men in the male ministry that could really share the gospel and never hesitated about it.

Hector invited me to his home to meet his wife and Alma became my big sister in Dallas. Hector was like a brother to me. When I had trouble with college math, he would take the time to help me understand and fussed the entire time. He would make sure I was safe when inclement weather headed our way. Alma would shake her head when we would argue and say, "You know how your brother is." God blessed me with them and after twelve years they never changed.

Doors kept opening the more I yielded to God's Spirit. I became the evangelism instructor for the church for over thirteen years. I was certain God was using this for something greater. Sometimes there were eighty new members and sometimes there were only two in monthly training. I didn't know what God was doing, but it wasn't my business. It was His. I knew I was working together with God according to Ephesians 2:10.

"For we are His workmanship, created in Christ Jesus for good works, which God prepared beforehand that we should walk in them."

I admit, there were many times I wanted to give up. The feeling would diminish as I would focus on the promises of God and bringing glory to him. Though our church was over 5000 members by then, the evangelism team consisted of only nine. The nine of us were truly a community. We were in each other's lives and learned to accept the good, bad, and indifferent about each other. We grew!

A blessed man of God once told me you always need a Paul in your life. One who cares for you like a surgeon yet loves you like a father. Everyone needs a Barnabas in their life. A great encourager that you could be real with. And everyone needs a Timothy in their life. One you can pour into and build up. Tan, a friend from New Orleans, was my Barnabas. For thirteen years, we spent holidays together preparing meals for those less fortunate and going under bridges praying for people and winning souls to Jesus. We were both foodies and we lived the character.

More doors opened. I was blessed to be the speaker at retreats and women's functions. For a year, I was the early morning voice of motivation for KEPX radio station out of San Diego owned by a Captain Lament. He gave me the name "Ms. Dynamite".

CHAPTER 12

WHAT IS GOD UP TO THIS TIME?

Racism was evident out in the country. I accepted a new position because I asked and God gave it to me, going back into the field as an independent agent selling cancer protection to farmers and homeowners in west Texas. I was usually so far out in the country that it was a 20–30-minute drive to a McDonalds to use the restroom, or I had to squat on the road.

The greater the blessings, the more doors open, the greater the test became. One time I walked up to a homeowner's door and a little girl about ten years old came to the door. "Mom, there's a nigger at the door."

125

My mouth fell open, but my heart reached out to her. This is what she was taught by her parents. It was tragic. That town had Ku Klux Klan marches on Sundays…in 2013. The two years I spent out that way, I truly saw my growth in Jesus. God used me to minister and pray for a few folks as I worked. I lived out there four days a week and returned home to Dallas on Thursdays. The money was outstanding. What most earn in a month, I sometimes earned in less than a week, and I was killing two birds with one stone. As I walked those dusty roads I shared Jesus with sinners, encouraged believers, and earned a decent income at the same time.

I decided to take some time off and, just as I downsized to a smaller place, I received the phone call no mother wants to get. My son Pete was taken to the hospital because of a car accident and was in the ICU. When I arrived, all I could say was, "NO Lord. Why Lord?" I was told he wouldn't make it. I was told he would never walk again, talk again, and if he ever came back, he would be in a vegetative state due to a traumatic brain injury.

Every day, I was there. Two of my sons and their father came to help for a few days. Church members and friends assisted me by sitting with him every day around the clock for forty-six days. Prayers came from everywhere. The doctor reminded me every day of what He wouldn't be able to do. I knew God as a healer because He healed me. So, I reminded God, not that He forgot. I knew He was faithful to his word. At the same time, I knew God was sovereign and He chose not to allow my son to return home at that moment. I was willing to trust Him. My son didn't know who I was. He called me "lady."

Around the seventeenth day after he left the ICU, I began to sing to him a song from the scriptures. Psalm 34 and he began to sing with me. After a day of singing that song, he sat up and said, "Hey mama. I love you, Mama."

All I could do was cry, "Hallelujah! Jesus reigns, Hallelujah!" My Jehovah Rapha. It was a long journey. The son they said would never walk again, walked out of that hospital and today is the best carpenter I know next to his dad. If you say it can't be done, God will prove you wrong. It's been a long road, but My God is faithful.

When it rains, it pours? After that, I was taking care of six people in my one-bedroom apartment. When he was released from the hospital, I housed my Pete, his wife, and my four grandchildren to help them get back on their feet while he healed. But eventually my funds were exhausted, and the conditions weren't favorable, so they left.

Jett, a young lady I'd ministered to years before, called to check on me. She knew of my struggles and was concerned. I have many spiritual daughters, but I believe God chose Jett to be quite special. We bonded after a retreat I spoke at in Tyler, Texas. Her husband was like a son and her kids called me GG. We walked and prayed together every morning on a nearby park for about a year.

Her words were, "Queen Mother, you need to drop that apartment and come live with us and rest." My pride jumped out like a jack rabbit.

Surely, I wasn't going to live with anyone so I responded, "Oh, no, I can't do that."

Words I spoke to her years prior were given back to me. "I think you should lay your pride down and pack your bags." Needless to say, I humbled myself and moved to Anna, Texas with Jett, who I called my Pumpkin, and her husband my SDB. I called it sixty minutes from civilization, but it was the best two years. I watched the epitome of a godly marriage through them. They strived to out-serve each other. They talked about everything, and I took note of the honor and respect that were present even the midst of a disagreement. Most times they never knew I was there.

I attempted to leave several times. However, upon their request, I remained there for two years. Though they were a refuge for me at a troubled time in my life, God used me to assist when Pumpkin became ill as well as being a comfort to her, a motherly figure in the absence of her own, who lived in Louisiana.

By then, our church had gone through some transitions. What had been one church for twenty years was divided into two churches. It was an ugly split and a distasteful sight for professing Christians. I was out of town when this happened. Upon my return, I spent so much time trying to encourage others to stay focused on living a life pleasing to God that I didn't see when Satan sent his little imps my way again.

I came to church one day after missing a few Sundays and was asked what I was doing there. Lord, here we go again. That time, I understood no weapon formed against me could prosper and every tongue that rose up against me would be condemned. Since I knew that, I was a bit hurt, I got over it quickly. Psalm 27 was real to me. "The Lord is my light and my salvation; whom shall I fear? The Lord is the strength of my life; of whom shall I be afraid?" I had no more temptation to fight with my fist as my dad had taught me. The Lord was my strength. I was not afraid. He was the stronghold of my life.

"When my enemies rose up against me, they would stumble, and they would fall." I was so certain of this. I knew God would vindicate me. I even prayed for mercy for my accusers. In times like those, I had a Savior. I was very sure my anchor held and gripped the solid rock. I stayed there until God led me to a safe haven at the Open Bible Fellowship. God led me to place my membership there as the man of God spoke healing words to my soul. I learned that storms often draw out of us something that a calm sea can't. Corrie Boom, author of Hiding Place, said, "In order to realize the worth of the anchor, you have to feel the stress of the storm."

CHAPTER 13

THE PIECES ARE COMING TOGETHER FINALLY

It's been forty years since I trusted Jesus as my Savior and surrendered to his Lordship. I've road mapped portions of my life to share insecurities I felt and didn't know were there:

My bitterness I couldn't admit I had. Protecting myself and my pride and seeking acceptance.

Since becoming a Christian, Daddy told me to say, "If the Lord wills" I will do this or that (James 4:15). When I left New Orleans for the second time, I boldly stated I'd never go back and live there. God knew my heart and my stubbornness. I would drive from Dallas in a heartbeat just to take my mother to lunch. If she called, I'd come, and she knew it. But to live there? No way. It was fifteen years since my dad had passed and my elder brother and I prayed that God would not allow Mother, eighty-three years old at the time, to pass away in the house alone. She took care of my wheelchair-bound brother and he would never know if she was sick or worse because he couldn't visit her room. We prayed constantly.

As it so happened the Lord willed that I return to Zambia for one last mission trip. I was headed back to Africa to serve those that were hungry for truth. Pumpkin and SDB wanted to come with me. That was the height of my world, so the answer was yes! We connected with Michael and it was on. This would be their first time out of the country for ministry. This time the goal was to raise $3500 for each of us. Our church had gone through a split, so the financial support wasn't there like it was before. However, the faithful supporters that were consistent for the fourteen times I went were a blessing to me and they showed it.

We sold dinners, did email lists, and what I said I'd never do. Sell plasma. Pumpkin and SDB were successful. I attempted but, my veins were too small. We didn't reach our goal financially, but we made it safely to Zambia. We were still able to raise the money to get our flights and food taken care of. For the first time, Michael separated us all and we had to bring the Word of God to different churches at the same time. God used us to speak into the lives of many.

Though I always enjoy equipping God's people, it was the most gut-wrenching time I had ever experienced. We brought baby clothes from America for a couple as requested and visited the couple to eat dinner. Two days later I was informed that the mother had medical complications after being admitted for false labor and sent home twice. The medical facilities weren't able to meet her medical needs and she and the baby died.

I went silent and burst into tears. Why, Lord? Why did you take such a beautiful vibrant soul? Why did you take this baby? A cloud hung over my head rest of the week, though we carried on with our work.

When we returned, I was just stepping foot on America's soil when I received a phone call from a government agency. Hurricane Michael had ripped through the panhandle of Florida terribly. "Can you be in Florida on Sunday?"

"Good Lord, yes!" I needed the money and "Dear God, I am asking you for six months out there because I can surely earn a quick $60k to relieve a debt I need to pay." I had been accepting disaster contracts since 2005 and I knew what people went through.

Panama City was a site for sore eyes after a category 5 with 160mph winds. The scope of my position was a public affairs specialist to increase awareness, and I enjoyed helping business owners in the manner in which we were trained. We walked the streets trying to locate what was left of the businesses in hopes of reaching some of the business owners.

My testing period wasn't over. It became more intense, although it seemed easier because I understood that everything touching my life must have God's permission and there was a purpose behind it. There was a lesson to learn in everything. God directed my steps, and I grew so much more with my work partner. I was challenged with her and I wasn't really that fond of her.

The Holy Spirit tested me, humbled me, and bid me to ask her forgiveness for my attitude toward her. She felt the same way about me. This is how God does it when you submit to him. I didn't know this lady, but today we stay connected and our time working together became sweet. We accepted each other though we didn't like each other's methods. Instead of trying to change each other, we decided to tell each other how we felt and get over it. We prayed together every morning before a two-hour drive to our work site and we checked each other's attitude when it was off track. We grew. I think I was happier because I passed my God given test, honored the Lord and, gained a friend! God rewarded me with friendships from afar that last forever. We still touch bases. Our common ground was Jesus.

CHAPTER 14

TOUGHEST YEAR OF MY LIFE

In January, 2018, we received news that our agency was affected by the government shutdown and we were scheduled to return home the following day. Before I left my hotel room to attend the final meeting, I spoke to Don, my best friend who'd been in my networking circle for over twenty years. He traveled with me and was my best male friend for that length of time. He was a giver. That day, he was troubled and heartbroken by a girl in the Caribbean who had taken advantage of him.

He was never one to initiate, but that morning he called to say how his life was worth nothing and how much he really loved me. He'd talked like that before and

I would pray with him, reminding him of who God said he was.

The following day, I arrived at the airport headed back to DFW at 6:00am and my cell phone rang. It was a mutual friend of ours. She asked, "Are you sitting?"

"Yes. I'm at the airport waiting to board."

"Our friend just took his life."

I yelled at the top of my voice, "Noooooo!" Stretched out on the airport seat, it came to me. The day before, he said goodbye and I hadn't caught it. No, God. Why? How?

This was the guy that called me every single morning for over twenty years to say, "Rise and shine Millionaire Woman of God." This was the guy who heard me speak at a networking convention and asked me to come help build his team in Augusta, GA, resulting in the fastest, largest team in the company. He believed in me like my dad did. This guy became like a little brother to me and everywhere I spoke, he was there.

One of my coworkers comforted me all the way to Dallas. After arriving home, I was unpacking and sobbing at the same time. The phone rang again. My uncle, my dad's brother, had just passed away. I couldn't stop the tears if I wanted to. The third phone call came through. I was afraid to answer. But it was only Rob, one of my travel partners. He knew I would drive to Atlanta, so he encouraged me to come home to New Orleans so he could drive us both to Don's service in Atlanta.

Upon my arrival, I shared with my mother what I was going through, and she did as mothers do, comforted me and bid us well on the road to his service. There were over 1000 people in attendance. How could that be, and no one recognized his fatal depression. I rode in disbelief all the way back to New Orleans.

I was going to head back to Dallas, but remember, I'm in tune to my steps being ordered by God. One of my agents noticed there was an event in Kenner, LA, and it would be worth attending. I hesitated but didn't say no. That put me there for a few extra days, so I stayed for my uncle's funeral. Mother had to sing. She did an incredible job as usual, but after the first stanza she began coughing. She finished the chorus, and the coughing resumed. My mother could scale a piano with her voice so this was disturbing to me.

On the way home she was still coughing, and I asked her to allow me to take her to the doctor. She refused, stating it was just a little inflammation and she was taking a seven-day prednisone pack prescribed a few days before. I begged my mother to let me take her, but she still refused. There was one thing I'd learned those past few years: God desires to hear from me especially when I need direction. According to Proverbs 3:5-6, He promised to show me the path.

I literally got prostrate in my room next to my mother and asked God to please turn her heart and allow me to take her to the doctor. I went to bed around 10pm. I kept waking up, calling on the name of the Lord.

"Lord, do something." Her cough was getting worse. Midnight, then 2am…nothing.

At exactly 4am, she called out to me. "Marian. Come take me to the hospital." I jumped up like a jack rabbit.

"Thank you, Father. I know you got this." When I entered her room she said she was hungry. "It's 4am, but ok, what do you want?"

"Just fix me a little something." I prepared grits, eggs, sausage, toast, and coffee. My mother isn't a breakfast person, but she ate every bit of it! I assisted her getting dressed and off to the ER. I wasn't nervous. I was just wondering what God was up to. They found all her levels were off. Her oxygen was low, her sugar was elevated, her blood pressure was high, but she was in good spirits and making all the nurses laugh. They admitted my mother for observation and to get her to a stable condition. I'd already resolved in my heart that I would come home to take care of her but I returned to Dallas to participate in a homeless event for the mayor.

I left Thursday, and my brother called me Friday saying my mom was dehydrated. On Friday, she wouldn't eat. Saturday, she was transferred to the ICU. And on Sunday, I was back in New Orleans at her bedside.

My mother's kidneys shut down, they found bone cancer plus she had battled with congestive heart failure for years. They offered her dialysis and chemo. Our answer was no and so was hers. "If the Lord is ready for me, I'm going. If he's not, I'll be here."

At her bedside, I asked her if she wanted to be buried with her hat (she was a hat lady).

"No, child, just make sure you put my wig on and my lipstick." I teared up but I didn't let them fall. Without the treatments, the doctors said she would only live three days. We brought her home to the hospice. A dear friend from church helped me care for her as I listened to her snoring each night. That Friday, she slept all day after the hospice nurse bathed her. In and out I could hear my mother but at 10:45pm I heard nothing. As I entered her room she was lying peacefully on her side.

Mother was gone.

That was the worst year of my life. Three deaths in two months. February 8, 2019, marked the day she left me.

Mother was buried just as she requested. Her will and obituary were already written, and she sang at her own funeral. My brothers and I had nothing to do but sign papers and grieve properly. I encourage you, my reader, to get your business in order for your family. It would be a gift of love to them.

I began to meditate on how everything had happened back at home, where I didn't want to be.

It hit me like a ton of bricks! God denied my request to stay in Panama City for six months to get rid of the debt I owed. Is that not his will to be debt free? Of course, it is. But I also prayed that my mother not die in her home alone.

My God. I burst into tears. "God you are so faithful you denied my request and granted my desire."

I thought I knew what I needed most, but God knew what I was able to handle. I was with Mother. Lord, I don't know what I would have done if my mother had passed away and I was in Panama City. Only God knows, and that's why he orchestrated it this way. I'm balling as I write this. Oh, how He loves me. He doesn't start anything that He doesn't finish. I'm now in great expectation once again.

My middle brother, Manny, and I took care of my brother Pie. If anyone knows the job of a caretaker, it's not the easiest thing, especially if the person isn't compliant. Pie has been in wheelchair over fifty-five years. I would cook for him and Manny would wash his clothes, keep room clean, and bath him. Sometimes, he wouldn't take his medicine as instructed, wouldn't stay out of the street in his wheelchair or listen to what I would ask him to do.

The year was passing quickly, and my faith was really being tested, but I was at a place in my faith walk where I was able to serve God because I want to. According to 1 Peter 4:10, I'm instructed to use whatever gift I have to serve others by putting God on display despite the way I feel. I was told when I was little that the Bible is basic instructions before leaving earth. I see it today fifty years later. I wish I could say I follow it totally, but I can't. However, I can say when I delight myself in him, he gives me the desires of my heart (Psalm 37:4). Like I said, God has a track record with me.

One day there was knock on the door. Someone hit my brother in his wheelchair. Except they didn't just hit him, they dragged him a block. When I got to the site, the wheelchair was smashed and all I could hear was him moaning. His frontal bone on his face was broken, his back was cracked, hip broken, and he had three punctured ribs and a severed bladder. Pie had surgery on his back and hip and was transferred to a nursing facility for a year before returning home where my two brothers and I took care of him.

Here we go again, Lord. It's this thing called my journey.

In addition to the problems with my brother, betrayal struck home when I received phone calls from friends across the state. They informed me that Brian stated across the world I was an estranged mother because I didn't support him singing R/B and all he ever wanted me to say was that I was proud of him. I cried so hard. My cousin tried to comfort me by telling me it was probably for the ratings, but that didn't comfort me at all.

Ratings at the expense of my character? My stomach knotted up. My head hurt for days. He said my family rejected him. Obviously, that wasn't true. Yes, it was a shock to everyone that he decided to sing R/B instead of gospel since that's where his roots came from. But being rejected, and I was estranged? No way. While following his dream after hurricane Katrina, he lived with my cousin at no charge in Atlanta for nearly a year. I talked to him weekly, if not more often than that. Every time he had a gig, he would call me, and I'd pray that God would allow him to do well. He said he was homeless and was misused by other popular artists. I put money in his account to make sure he ate.

I sacrificed everything I had to help make his dreams come true. And I was estranged? My child was eating with me the night he made his big debut. We had already scheduled for me to visit and cook for him for a week after Mom passed away in 2019. I'd already purchased tickets to get there, and I carried it out even in pain. My child talked to me to let me know he couldn't make his grandmother's funeral because he was on tour out of the country. Only people from New Orleans who were with us from the very beginning and those across the states that I had praying for him knew his words weren't true.

The Bible says the words of a talebearer are like stabbing deep inside your belly (Proverbs 18:8). I felt like someone was stabbing me in my heart over and over again. All the other tests I had were endurable, but I wasn't sure I would survive that one until God spoke deep in my Spirit again: Nothing touches you without my permission. I will be glorified. I will vindicate you. No need to fight, this battle of pain, embarrassment, and betrayal is mine (2 Chronicles 20:15).

I had to remember again. It's not my son, it's the work of Satan. His job is to steal, kill, and destroy. In this season of my life Satan wanted to destroy me because of how God plans to use me to expand his kingdom. A calm came over me like none other.

While all of this was going on I was communicating weekly with my son like I had with all of them through text or phone. It felt like a bad story. Honestly, we have never been estranged and are not estranged today. We meet as a family for holidays on zoom calls and regular text.

We don't talk as often on the phone like we use to, but when we do it's for hours. He knows I love him and God knows I forgive him. When I confronted him once about it, his response was," It's my job, so don't believe all of that." As I have looked at all of this from God's perspective and asked why, God reminded me again that He is in control, and He is working the plan for my good (Romans 8:28).

CHAPTER 15

PANDEMIC REVEALS PURPOSE

Couldn't God have allowed something else rather than a pandemic? In March 2020, COVID-19 hit our nation. In the first week there were 140 cases in Louisiana alone. We were told not to go outside, to avoid people, and to wear masks. Because of my work assisting families and businesses financially, I was always around people. Most of my business I was able to conduct on the phone and via the internet. After the first two weeks I was beginning to get comfortable.

I spent more time in God's presence and had certainty and confidence that He would protect me. I stood on this promise and am still standing. I remained in this secret place knowing He would protect me. There were so many deaths around me. Five of my classmates died, another uncle passed away, and a few close family members and friends contracted the virus and suffered greatly.

It was during this quiet season that God slowly began allowing me to map my life. This pandemic drew my family closer together. I was already communicating with my sons and their father, but it became even more frequent. On the Fourth of July, 2020, we shared a beautiful time outside, socially distanced, and masked. Because I see everything from God's perspective and through His eyes today, deep in my gut I was able to see that God had allowed this pandemic to draw me closer to Him. I fell in Love with Jesus all over again as I took a closer look at my life and where He'd brought me from. God was saying to me, "Do you love me for who I am or what I've done?"

God, I love You for who You are. And I am so grateful for what You have done. Lord, You are a sovereign God. You do as you will, when You will, and with whom You will. I'm just asking, where to now? What now? It's been two and a half years since my mother passed and I am debt free. I'm still waiting to complete my mother's estate business. My brother is still in the hospital. I am really to leave. I don't know. Speak Father.

The phone rang and I was thinking it was another death. They were coming readily. It wasn't. Harry was calling to check on me. We'd been doing that often since the start of the pandemic. Our conversation was about how much we appreciated each other and past issues that have made us into who we are today. I believe this particular day we were sharing our devotions. Out of the blue-sky Harry said to me, "You know I never cheated on you right?" Instead of going into a defensive fight mode, I was startled. He repeated himself.

Now I had the biggest why for God than I ever had before. I asked, "Do you believe I had every reason to think you were?"

He responded "Yes."

"Well, I'm glad you told me so. That's a relief." At that moment all I could ask within myself was "Why? Why didn't you say the evidence I had was untrue?" I only voiced that silently.

I wasn't angry, just confused. I needed to know why since I'd planned to be married to one man, one time until I died. I tried to be angry, but the emotions would only come as pain and confusion. I just needed to know from God... Why?

CHAPTER 16

FREEDOM IS NEAR AND HERE IS WHY?

Sometimes when you get answers, you feel relief, but I still had a lot of questions for God since my steps were ordered by him. I know God isn't obligated to tell me everything, I'm his creature (Psalm 100:3). But Lord, why am I happy and confused at the same time? I was in great expectation to hear God answer all my whys, and I know you are, too.

Fredrick Douglas said it best. "There is no progress without a struggle."

In the words of Marian Brown, God said, "I created you. I formed you before the foundation of this world. Even in your mother's womb, I knew you. I loved you then and I wanted you to grow up to be a woman set apart for me. I wanted you to be used as a vessel to accomplish some things here on earth. I wanted you to be virtuous and help others through your boldness, transparency, and honesty. I wanted you to have compassion with others and know how to serve them. I wanted you to encourage those who were sick and saw no hope. I wanted people to be able to come to you for advice and you point them to Me."

"I wanted you to encourage the broken hearted, to set people free. I wanted you to be able to share my love with those that had been rejected, betrayed, and scorned. I needed you to be prepared to encourage single mothers that were bitter. I wanted you to be able to fight as your dad taught you, but now with the truth. Oh, daughter of the Most High God, you were none of that."

"When you were born, you were a busy little one and a smart-mouth most times. You were born into a family of men, and that was my plan. I brought your sister into your life because your little heart always cried for one. Do you remember? You were born caring, but I needed to transform you because you were selfish at times. You had a strong personality. You were always confident. I used your father for that, but it turned sour because you rebelled. I allowed you to take note of your parents' hard work because I knew it would form good habits in you."

"When you went to California, my child, you were headed for destruction. I was there the whole time. I knew you would destroy yourself. I couldn't allow you to be successful in modeling, though my heart cried when Victor raped you. My child, it was not a good experience for you. It took you a few years, but I am happy you forgave him. I heard you when you prayed for his soul's salvation. I love you, my child. Because that happened to you, you were able to help the little girls who had been molested and raped in Africa. Do you remember the freedom those girls received the day you and Bee ministered to them? They were shouting, 'Hallelujah! Hallelujah!'"

"My dear daughter, I don't waste anything. I use everything, even the bad. When I found you, you battled so much, you fought so hard to convince yourself you had a relationship with me. You were faithfully in church but so far from me. I was so happy you accepted my love for you by trusting my Son. I threw a party for you and all the angels were here. We were all so happy. I saw your heart after I saved you. You needed to see I will always love you, but you needed transformation because the beast of immorality was waiting for you.

I allowed you to love Harry hard. I needed you to know what rejection felt like. You doubted his leadership because of the areas he lacked in. You were still supposed to trust him but you didn't. My plan was to bring hurting women in your pathway. The only way you would be able help them is to be able to relate to them. You had to go through this my child. I allowed you to go to the cult because it was there that you learned the power of my Word that was going to keep you. You learned how to serve from your parents. It was in the cult that I taught you to master it and now you do it willingly. I watch you. You love it. The seven years you stayed there was my number of perfection. You told me you never wanted to fall into adultery or fornication again. My dear, you needed my Word. I knew you were sincere when you asked me to kill you if you ever did it."

"See, my child, I've kept you. It's been twenty-five years and my word still works. Don't think for one moment that you are perfect, but you have grown and I am proud of you. About your illness, once again, my child, I waste nothing. I needed you to know me as a healer and encourage others. I heard you as you referenced how I healed you when you prayed for your son. You prayed so hard. I needed you to know how to pray for others and stand on my Word with them. During that time, you developed a healthy lifestyle and look at you my child. Today, you are helping many people safely get off medications because you have traveled that road.

"Are you beginning to understand? My child, are you really paying attention to your life? You had been close to your dad, and you kept praying to have a closer relationship with your mom. My child if I had not taken your dad your prayers would have never been answered. Did I not answer? You had the most beautiful five years with your mother as an adult until I took her. You prayed to be with your mom when she died. I granted that for you. You have been faithful in my word. Did I not say, "If you abide in me and my words abide in you, you can ask whatever you want, and I will do it so that the Father can be glorified." You kept telling everyone about how I answered that prayer for you. I inhabited your praise. You put me on display.

"I believe I have proven myself to you over and over. This is your journey my child. Nothing is wasted. I needed you to see yourself, if you really did trust that I had you covered. I needed to see you obey Matthew 5:43-48. You called on me to help you maintain when you read the lies told on you. Dear Child, that means nothing. It's Brian's journey and you are in it. Do you not believe a lie is only for a moment (Proverbs 12:19)? I used it so that you could help other parents with the importance of learning what each of their children may need and not place them in places where only I belong.

"Oh, my child, I will honor your sacrifice. Have I ever forsaken you? You made it through. My words tell you, if you live godly, it's a guarantee you will suffer persecution for my sake. Many times, you creatures suffer for your own foolishness. Most of those things that happen to you were the consequences of your own choices. I made good out of them because you love me and are called for my purpose. I knew you before you were born, and I chose you to become like me. But you have a very long way to go."

"There are more tests, big and small, but more blessings, too. Blessings far more than what you can ever imagine are in the atmosphere. My daughter, as you share with others you are reaching inside of yourself. As you give to them, I will give good measure back to you. I am bringing you from glory to glory and it costs.

"The pandemic touched your life to draw you closer to me. I make no apologies for it. Because of it, you and your family became closer. They were able to see your growth and so were you. You made some unwise choices but despite them all, I ordered your steps. Remember the Beautiful Gate (Acts 3:1-16). A cripple was brought there daily to ask for money. This gate was known for the richness of metal it was made of and its curious workmanship. People came through to be healed. When Peter and John entered the gate, the cripple asked them for money. Peter told the man, 'Silver and gold I do not have, but I will give you what I have in the name of Jesus Christ of Nazareth. Rise up and walk.' Do you recall that my child? You are that Gate. I called you for something different, something special. People talk to you and are encouraged. Some have been made aware and some are on their way to freedom. You understand that I am good to the just and good to the unjust. You understand that and treat people as I would. This was all about teaching you to become more like me. I created you in my image so that you can bring Me glory.

Let me remind you I spoke to you through a quote you read years ago: "People come into your life for seasons, reasons, or lifetimes."

Seasons to make you laugh, smile, or to encourage you to do something you have never done before. And then they are gone. Reasons, because you have expressed a need or something emotional, physical, or spiritual. That need was met, and then they were gone. Lifetimes. Those people are to teach you lifelong lessons because they are with you forever. You must love them, accept them, and use their relationship to build another one.

So, rejoice, my child, your journey has just begun.

"I had you fall in love with journaling and allowed the pandemic so you can tell this story you have put off over thirteen years to help this reader. They are getting the picture right this very moment. They are mapping over their lives right now, and because of your story, many will be free. I don't waste anything, my child."

CHAPTER 17

THIS IS WHO YOU REALLY ARE

Today, I know who I am. I am a masterpiece created by God almighty. I am strong. I am confident. I am who God says I am , and I couldn't keep saying the opposite of what God says about me. Now dear reader, allow me to speak to you. If God says you're strong, why do you keep saying, "Lord, I'm so weak"? You can change those words to express your emotion and declare the truth. "Lord, I'm feeling weak, but I know I'm strong." So, the first thing we are going to focus on is changing our words. Let the weak say, I am strong (Joel 3:10).

We always say the devil did this or that. But keep in mind we have four enemies, and they are satan, your flesh, the world, and the greatest one, yourself. When God showed me how easily I sabotaged myself, I had to begin taking ownership and cleaning house. Today, I am secure in him. I am approved by God, and I need no one else's validation to feel worthy. My worth comes from Him.

We are all products of our environment. Therefore, you must look closely through prayer at things in your past life that affected you negatively. This cannot be done alone, you need help. Ask God to help you.

1. Face your past by voicing it and embracing it. Make two columns on a page. On the left, write down all the challenging or negative things that were done to you by yourself or someone else, and all the negative things you have done to others. On the right side of the paper, write all the things you desire to be and that you are. Confident, strong, protected, determined, etc. Write who God says you are.

Forgiven, more than a conqueror, faithful, righteous, strong, mighty, etc. Whether you feel or see them, you must say them out loud daily.

2. Take responsibility for your own actions and forgive yourself. In other words, we're not looking at the actions of anyone else but yours. Make no excuses for why you did a thing. Take full responsibility. And answer these questions on another sheet of paper: What could I have done to make this better? What was my error? What was my failure? What can I do now to make going forward better? Focus on changing you. That's the only person you can change.

3. Actually, make the changes. Example, if that means you need to call someone that hurt you, do so. Tell them why you're offended and how they hurt you. If they don't respond properly, you have released them. If they do respond properly, you have still released them. Remember, the person you are changing is you. You're not responsible for the other person's actions. When you return to your place of solitude, you can

begin to thank God for giving you back your peace. The Bible says a person offended is harder to be won than a strong city and their contentions are like the bars of a castle (Proverbs 18:19). That's strong! But by God's grace you can do it. Remember what God says, you are more than a conqueror through Him (Romans 8:37). Every day, pray for that person. God will bless them; your burden and pain will diminish. You'll find your compassion increasing. It will take a while, but you're on your way to freedom.

4. If you're stuck in your own past and blaming everyone for your present state, you must do the same. Ask God to forgive you for not forgiving yourself. You must face and voice your uncomfortable past. You must embrace that it happened. You must look at that sheet of paper you wrote on and decide where you want to stay. On the right side or the left? In the past, I've had accountability partners to remind and encourage me until I'm able to encourage myself. If your accountability partner reminds you of who you

are now but if you decide to continue to rehearse the past, you haven't truly taken responsibility. You're lying to yourself.

Will this happen overnight? No, it won't. But if you follow these simple steps sincerely, you'll be further than you were before you started reading this book. It's like this: You're about to get married. You stand before the preacher, say the vows, and the preacher says the words, "I now pronounce you man and wife." Y'all walk out, go on a honeymoon, or back home and live married lives. What was different? The preacher only "pronounced" you man and wife. He said you are man and wife and you begin to live a married life that was different from your life before. You made changes.

So once you have faced your past, taken responsibility, and forgiven yourself as well as forgiven others, make the changes and take own it . Through your relationship with God, you have been declared free. You're free, my friend. Live free. You've made the changes. The Bible says let not sin have control and have power over you (Romans 6:14). God has given you everything you need to beat it. If you don't, it's on you.

I'll never forget the first time I saw "Diary of a Mad Black Woman" in 2005. I thought, surely, that's not who I was or how I felt, but it was. It was the story of a prominent black attorney who abused his wife. She got revenge until she realized the power of bitterness and the damage it causes. I saw myself in this movie. A bitter black woman. I didn't want to admit the bad things I'd wanted to happen to those that hurt me. Praise God, By the grace of God I saw my own condition and fixed it!

If I had to do this all over again, here's what I would change. First, I would recognize that I can't take everybody with me on my journey. See I love relationships. I always thought that if you found a friend, that person should be with you forever. Zia K Abdelnour said it best, "Life is like an elevator. On your way up, sometimes you have to stop and let some people off." I had to accept that not everyone would like me and not everyone was for me. I was funny, confident, witty, smart, I love Jesus, but guess what? Not everyone likes Marian.

One Sunday, Bishop Jakes, from The TD Jakes Show, shared that there are three types of people around you. This was an eye opener for me and an emotional life saver. It helped me to see and accept people for who they are and their purpose in my life. Because I was the type of person to want everybody to do better, be better, I would often try to help them reach potential without being asked to do so. I accepted every person I met as a friend even if I just met them. When I learned about the three types of people that surround you, it gave me freedom once again.

Those people are:

1. Constituents - these people are with you because they're interested in what you stand for. They stand for what you stand for. They don't really like you.

2. Comrades - those that are against what you are against. Y'all have the same enemy. Once the battle is won and the enemy is down, they're gone. They don't like you, either.

3. Confidants - they'll be with you in rain, snow, sleet, or shine. Confidants will tell you about yourself because they love you. They'll be by your side through thick or thin.

Bishop Jakes also shared a parable called "The Giraffe and The Turtle." He shared so profoundly how the giraffe eats from the tops of trees and the turtle eats and moves in the grass. We can be in the same location and not have the same view. He shares how we, as human beings, eat on the level of our vision. When I had a vision, being the giraffe I am, I would share it with a friend that had a turtle view. They could only see from the level they were on. Nothing was wrong with the turtle but he was responding from his perspective. I learned to be cautious about who I tell my dreams to. Sometimes they would speak the truth about my past. But they defined me by the way I used to be and had no clue who I am today.

The giraffe has a twenty-five-pound heart so that it can pump blood into its nine-foot neck. His head must stay high. If he lowers his head too low to eat, it will cut off his oxygen and he'll pass out. When you're built to be tall, you'll endanger your position if you lower your perspective. The turtle isn't wrong, he's just reporting on his level. He can't reach up, so you can't explain a giraffe decision to the turtle.

If I had to start this journey over, I'd incorporate those two points into my life. I wouldn't decide to take everyone with me and I wouldn't tell everyone my dreams. Everything else would stay the same, even the pain and trials I endured. I discovered my why, and my

God wasted nothing. God was preparing me for this time going forward. "Thank you Father" is my continued praise.

You've made it to the end of my story, but the beginning of your healing. Just as you have read my story, take the necessary steps to bring healing to your well-being and create another story of healing balm for the world. If you need a bit of encouragement or would like to sponsor a "Bondage to Freedom Workshop" for your small group, church or organization, drop me a line at ourfreedomishere@gmail.com. You can also hear the stories of others who are growing on their life journeys. Real topics, real people, real talk on my YouTube channel every Sunday 6pm CST.

https://youtube.com/channel/UCTYzOb1eLhmX3o7f
t9jmITQ

End

Made in the USA
Coppell, TX
11 November 2021